KNOW YOUR
VALUE

ALSO BY MIKA BRZEZINSKI

Grow Your Value: Living and Working to Your Full Potential

Obsessed: America's Food Addiction—and My Own

All Things at Once

MIKA BRZEZINSKI

KNOW YOUR
VALUE

WOMEN, MONEY, AND
GETTING WHAT YOU'RE WORTH

REVISED EDITION

hachette
BOOKS

NEW YORK   BOSTON

The survey mentioned in the original introduction was conducted online within the United States by Harris Interactive on behalf of MSNBC from August 25–27, 2010, among 2,273 adults ages 18 and older. This online survey is not based on a probability sample and therefore no estimate of theoretical sampling error can be calculated. For complete survey methodology, including weighting variables, please contact www.harrisinteractive.com.

Hachette Books
Hachette Book Group
1290 Avenue of the Americas, New York, NY 10104
hachettebooks.com
twitter.com/hachettebooks

Originally published in hardcover and ebook by Weinstein Books in April 2011. Paperback conversion by Weinstein Books in April 2012. First revised and updated hardcover edition published by Hachette Books September 2018.

Hachette Books is a division of Hachette Book Group, Inc. The Hachette Books name and logo are trademarks of Hachette Book Group, Inc.

The publisher is not responsible for websites (or their content) that are not owned by the publisher.

The Hachette Speakers Bureau provides a wide range of authors for speaking events. To find out more, go to www.hachettespeakersbureau.com or call (866) 376-6591.

Editorial production by Christine Marra, *Marra*thon Production Services. www.marrathoneditorial.org

Library of Congress Control Number: 2018942030

ISBN 978-1-60286-594-5 (revised hardcover); ISBN 978-1-60286-595-2 (revised ebook);
ISBN 978-1-60286-134-3 (original hardcover); ISBN 978-1-60286-142-8 (original ebook);
ISBN 978-1-60286-160-2 (trade paperback)

Printed in the United States of America
LSC-H

10 9 8 7 6 5 4 3 2 1

FOR MY GIRLS,
EMILIE AND CARLIE

I love you,
Mom

CONTENTS

ACKNOWLEDGMENTS

A special thank you to my friend, Rachel Campbell, who has made everything in my life possible, including this book, with her valuable insights, patience, and guidance through turbulent times. Your friendship never waivers even when there are hurricane-force winds! To Rachel and her husband, Dave, thank you both for your friendship, love, and unconditional support.

Also, a heartfelt thank you to the extraordinary women (and men) whom I interviewed for sharing their invaluable time and insights with me.

I'd like to thank Emily Cassidy for being my editor on the re-release of this book; you worked tirelessly to make sure we got this right. There is no one I trust more to help me share my truth, and your ability to see the big picture has made you indispensable.

Also, thank you to Janet Klein for collaborating on the entire concept and content of the original manuscript. We needed to make some changes, but the core of what was written here has withstood the test of time.

Putting it together has been a learning experience for everyone involved. Special thanks to Amanda Murray and Georgina Levitt. You have always been supportive of my ideas, and I am thankful to be able to continue to work with you.

I'd like to thank Andy Lack, Phil Griffin, Steve Burke, Brian Roberts, David Cohen, and everyone in my Comcast NBCUniversal family for supporting *Morning Joe* . . . and also providing a vibrant, robust platform for *Know Your Value.*

Know Your Value started with my story, which I soon realized was universal.

It is my passion to teach all women to know their value AND to communicate it effectively and NOT to make the many mistakes that I made. Since I was sharing my experience at work . . . I thought "my bosses will never let this happen." That was not the case . . .

Phil Griffin . . . you stepped up and took yet another chance on us and Comcast was right there backing you up.

Thank you Shawn Leavitt and Vicki Neidigh for helping me realize this vision—and being as obsessed with it as me.

Thank you to Jared DiPalma for doing and re-doing the math.

These are leaders who see the value in giving women their voices and showing them how to own it and win.

Duby McDowell, Robyn Gengras, and Diane Smith, you have been with me from the start.

And Jane Kaupp, who has taken the baton and run with it.

To Luna Szoke, Ashling Stanek, Kalee Hearing, Maureen Clancy, and Lesley Stevenson: thank you for your help transcribing and organizing so many of the amazing interviews. I am so glad to have you all on my team and I can't wait to watch your careers continue to grow and blossom.

And now for the two biggest reasons I wrote this book: my girls. I thank my daughters for inspiring me every day to share this message with other women. Emilie and Carlie, I want the sky to be the limit for both of you in life. Know your value. Mommy truly does.

A KNOW YOUR VALUE MOMENT, ALMOST MISSED

Know Your Value has become so much more than a book since its original release in 2011.

So many women got raises after reading this book. Countless women have stopped me on the street or at airports across the country to say these exact eight words: "I read your book. I got a raise!" And then they hug me. And while I am not usually a hugger of strangers, when I hear those words I hug back. Sometimes I tear up.

This book is more than a guide to negotiating your salary. I wrote it to teach women how to dig deep, find their own voices, and communicate their value effectively. The book is about getting your full value in every relationship: at work, at home, in life. I show women how apologizing and self-deprecating actually depreciates their value at the very moment they should be cashing in. This is as much a "what to do" book as it is a "what not to do" guide, with my mistakes as exhibits A, B, C, and D in full view—once again, warts and all. This book is about how to get more money, more recognition, more respect for your contributions . . . how to get your true value.

I'm proud of the women who have taken the advice in this book to heart, because I know it's not just about the money; it is the Know Your Value process that has paid off in their paychecks . . . and their lives. I am so thrilled when I see that light in their eyes, that victorious posture, and that energy. They read the book and the advice I gathered here from so many strong, fascinating women. My readers put themselves out there, and they set their lives on a whole different path forward with endless possibilities that simply did not exist in their minds before.

The book has inspired a conference series, a multiplatform social media effort, and there are more books in the works. We have taken the Know Your Value message on the road to cities across the country and have helped thousands of women know and grow their value. We have brought aspirational and inspirational women together to have conversations about how we as women can get our worth in all areas of our lives.

THE INSPIRATION for the first edition of this book occurred on a beautiful spring day back in 2010. I was in the White House and dropped by presidential advisor Valerie Jarrett's office to say hello. We started talking about work-life balance. We discussed the excitement and challenges of having so many opportunities as women. For Valerie, the challenges were raising an incredible daughter on her own, navigating the worlds of business and politics at the top level, and helping to propel the first African-American president into office. For me, they were raising two extraordinary girls while traveling the country and covering the Obama presidency. We marveled at all that was possible, but also commiserated about the cost of our choices. The sacrifice. The determination that meeting our challenges required. I had just written a memoir, and I mentioned that I had an idea for another book, but I didn't think my schedule would allow me to write it. I could barely do any of my jobs well. I was wavering about whether I could handle the workload along with the three-hour morning show.

She asked what the concept was, and I described to her my theories about women and value. I explained how poorly I'd advocated for myself over the course of my career, and what I'd learned recently about how I could have earned so much more—not just more money, but more recognition for my contributions—and how I had talked to so many successful women who admitted to floundering the same way. I realized immediately that I'd hit a nerve. She said, "You have to write this book. This is important. This is the next part of the conversation. Even more, this book is in you. You have to write it. It's so important." Her eyes locked in, dead serious.

And then she proceeded to tell me about the White House Council on Women and Girls, and its efforts for National Equal Pay Day, the Lilly Ledbetter Fair Pay Act, the Paycheck Fairness Act, and all the studies they had underway. She told me the administration had people at every level dealing with women's issues, whether it be access to capital or the gender wage gap. Valerie not only urged me to write the book, she said, "I'll help you. What can I do? We've gotten really far. Women run the world. But we're not getting our value."

Valerie Jarrett was an inspiration to me and a catalyst for this project. What really was just a casual visit had taken a dramatic turn, and I walked out of her office knowing I was going to write this book. I realized that if my story spoke to Valerie, then it certainly would speak to others.

FAST FORWARD TO 2017: The world is a different place.

Soon after his inauguration, Donald Trump invited me and Joe Scarborough to Sunday lunch at the White House. I could see immediately how swept up he was in his new job. Instead of feeling the weight of responsibility that any sane leader would feel upon his shoulders, Trump was like a kid in a candy shop who was giddy with his new surroundings.

"He's gone. What few guardrails he allowed to be put up during the campaign are completely gone now. He is about to get worse than ever," Joe had observed after talking with him on inauguration night.

Before the White House lunch, Ivanka Trump and I discussed the importance of getting the new president to focus on the kind of women's issues that I had worked on with Valerie Jarrett throughout the Obama administration. Because it was so difficult to get Donald Trump to focus on any topic that did not feed directly into his ego, Ivanka and I discussed strategies to break through Trump's flurry of self-aggrandizing stories and fog of disinterest.

After lunch, I stood up to go look at the desserts as an excuse to interrupt his constant droning on about his election win, the record size of his inaugural crowd, and how great his first week in the White House had been. Of course, his first week was *not* great and the crowd at his inauguration a week earlier was far smaller than Barack Obama's. The fact that Joe and I had already pointed out both of those facts to him probably did nothing to put our relationship back on positive footing, but I wasn't done trying. As I got up and moved toward a side table, I turned around and said, "Donald, we need to talk about women's issues."

"What?" the president said.

"We need to talk about women's issues."

"Huh?"

"Women, Donald, women! You know . . ."

I then motioned with my arms an hourglass figure in the air to re-late the topic to a man who clearly did not have a clue and did not care about the issues I had been discussing with Ivanka.

"Donald! I said WOMEN!" I felt dirty making the hourglass mo-tion, but it was the only way to get this misogynist to understand the word. Ivanka leaned forward.

Trump responded by looking at Ivanka condescendingly. "Oh yeah, women. Yeah honey, yeah, we will get to that." Just as quickly he moved on to talk about his travel ban. I glanced over at the pres-ident's daughter, who looked deflated as the conversation veered off to extreme vetting. It was clear that the man who spent years running beauty pageants and talking about women mainly in the context of their physical features was never going to see females as anything more than sex objects to rate on Howard Stern's show, or as the subject of locker room talk.

Not long after this lunch, the president of the United States would be attacking *my* looks via Twitter, accusing me of meeting with him while "bleeding badly from a facelift." It was a ludicrous tweet. The social media universe rose up to defend me, but I wasn't upset—until I remembered that Trump was quoted in the original *Know Your Value*, talking about how much he valued women!

Clearly it was time to revisit my book. Especially since my pub-lisher was . . . Harvey Weinstein (you can't make this stuff up). By the time I started writing this new edition, Harvey Weinstein had been revealed as an extraordinary abuser of women, and his downfall had sparked a worldwide movement. Women across the country—even across the globe—had had enough. The women's movement has been invigorated in ways that will play out in many elections to come.

Women were raising their voices and demanding equal treatment, equal pay, and to be heard in cases of sexual harrassment and assault. The #MeToo movement has changed the way we talk about office politics and appropriate professional relationships. We are now talking about abuse of power and the struggles women go through on the national stage. Women have been literally taking to the streets, fighting to be heard.

Once you truly own your voice, it's amazing how effective you can be with it.

While the rise of Donald Trump and the fall of Harvey Weinstein were catalysts for the re-release of this book, there were a number of other reasons I needed to revisit these pages. Professional and personal changes have given me new insight to share and inspired new questions to ask other women.

Morning Joe has become a fixture in the political landscape, the place where power players come to be a part of the national conversation. We are marking eleven years in 2018 with Joe, Willie Geist, and me as the longest-running anchor team on TV, and our ratings have never been better. We are reaching more people every single day, and that growth has taught me so much. These turbulent times have made it important for me to take everything we have written and update it, go deeper, and design it for today's world.

On top of the professional successes of *Morning Joe*, my personal life—which has become increasingly more public in the last few years—has gone through dramatic changes that have given me new insight into my own worth. I have been divorced and I am getting re-married. And while it is extremely important to me that I be respectful of all parties in what I do and do not share, I have learned so much since first writing this book about what it means to know your value . . . in all areas of your life. I discovered the message truly applies to your personal brand as well as your professional one.

The original book was successful in part because it included stunningly candid conversations with successful women who were willing to be interviewed on what, for many, can be a very personal subject. We have influential women in government such as Brooksley Born,

Sheila Bair, and Elizabeth Warren; personal-finance expert Suze Orman; media entrepreneurs Arianna Huffington and Tina Brown; and women's magazine leaders like *More* magazine's Lesley Jane Seymour and *Cosmopolitan*'s Kate White. I interviewed the unforgettable Nora Ephron, who passed away after the original publication, Joy Behar, and Susie Essman. I spoke to top researchers on the subject of gender and negotiation, such as Harvard's Hannah Riley Bowles. For the male perspective, I asked the likes of Jack Welch, Phil Griffin, Joe Scarborough, and Donny Deutsch to weigh in. Some of the interviewees had been on the show; some, like Facebook COO Sheryl Sandberg and Yahoo! CEO Carol Bartz, I thought should be on the show.

And now we've added some new voices we wanted to hear from and new research and statistics that are important to share. For this re-release, I brought fresh voices to the table such as former Director of the White House Domestic Policy Council and assistant to President Obama Melody Barnes, BBC World News presenter Katty Kay, and senior correspondent and editor on gender issues for the *New York Times* Susan Chira. Katty Kay has since broken through with *The Confidence Code* (her incredible book series) and joined forces with women at the BBC to expose pay inequality there. (Way to go, Katty!) And because I am proud of my network and the talented women who fill the airwaves, I spoke to Katy Tur, who anchors MSNBC Live and covered the Donald Trump campaign for the network as its campaign embedded reporter, political correspondent Kasie Hunt, and *Your Business* host JJ Ramberg. I also interviewed two of the women who were chosen as finalists in my national Know Your Value events, Jennifer Hotchkiss and Ashton Whitmoyer, because their stories resonated with me on both a deeply personal and professional level. I also spoke with former federal law enforcement officer and one of the top body language experts in the world, Janine Driver, who knocked our socks off at the last KYV event in New York City. She will make you look at your "looks" in a whole new way. I spoke with Joe Scarborough and re-interviewed

Phil Griffin. We added reproductive psychiatrist Dr. Catherine Birndorf, Executive Director of the Women and Public Policy Program at Harvard Victoria Budson, Executive Coach Liz Bentley, and SVP and CHRO at Independence Blue Cross Jeanie Heffernan.

The women I interviewed manage multibillion-dollar companies, run our government, and oversee our economy. These are women who deal day to day with challenges of national importance, yet I was struck by how similar our psychology was as we shared our experiences in the workplace. I assumed that such successful women must somehow have been smarter about their careers and their money. They must have taken a different road—we couldn't possibly have made similar mistakes. But as I began sharing my struggles with women in a variety of fields, many of them told me of their own troubled efforts to get a raise, earn a promotion, or just to have their ideas heard in the conference room. Why are things that seem to be simple for many men so difficult for many women? Why do we undermine ourselves, often right from the start? How have they managed to be compensated for their true value? What have they done wrong, and what have they done right? How do they balance their personal and professional lives to achieve their true value?

There are lessons to be learned from my experience with President Trump and his ridiculous tweets, the Harvey Weinstein mess, and from the experiences of a number of far more successful women I spoke with when writing this book.

And all the questions are answered when a woman knows her value.

For the women who I turn to in this book, about how they did it, their answers were surprisingly honest and unexpectedly revealing. Apparently none of them played the game exactly the way the men did. Among other things, they taught me some important lessons about getting out of my own way, learning to speak up, negotiating from a place of power instead of fear, owning my success, and perhaps most important, getting the compensation I deserve.

After all, there's money to be made in these lessons. And the lessons apply to everything in life. Money, in this book, is simply a metaphor. This is about being valued in the way you should be—at work or anywhere. Every lesson that you will read about in this book can apply to relationships, raising children, marriage, being in a profession, being in an industry, changing jobs . . . everything. Because if you don't demand what you're worth and you don't communicate it well, you won't be treated fairly, and the relationship will ultimately die.

And if you don't ask for what you deserve, you won't ever find out what you're made of, and what you truly can do. You undermine yourself by not developing your tools and learning what to do with them (and what not to do with them); how to use your voice, your brain, your words, your style, your approach, your finesse—everything in your power to get your value.

The issue of equal pay, the gender wage gap, knowing your value—these are perennially important issues that affect women everywhere. And in an age where women feel they have taken a massive step back every time they turn on the news and hear their president speak, equal pay is an issue that's more timely than ever, and truly affects everyone.

There are a variety of reasons for gender inequality in the workplace. Many of them are complicated, and some are not completely understood. But in sharing these cautionary tales and personal victories, research, and anecdotal evidence, I hope women will learn something that helps them chart their own course. I don't claim that we will eliminate the gender wage gap—not even close. But we can strategize and do much better for ourselves, and for the next generation. We are going to talk about your value to your company, your value to your family, and the cultural climate that surrounds these issues. What I've learned from the women I've interviewed will stay with me. I want to share their wisdom with my daughters, and in this book I will share their wisdom with you.

CHAPTER 1

SUCCESS, FAILURE, AND KNOWING YOUR VALUE

How It All Began

February 2008

About a decade ago, I was ready to walk away from it all. If I had quit that cold morning back in 2008, I would have walked away from a transformational show that has now chronicled a decade of politics. I would have missed reporting on one of the most fascinating political shifts of our lifetime, the two-party system blown to bits by broken promises from Bush, Bill, Hillary . . . and ultimately The Donald himself. What I also didn't know then was that I would have walked away from the man who I would ultimately fall in love with and promise to marry. Talk about unexpected twists! But when I turn back to this point in time, the story then was all about money, and I was taking it extremely personally.

JOE SCARBOROUGH SAT ACROSS FROM me in the windowed café at the bottom of Rockefeller Center. Outside, the rink was filled with bundled-up skaters enjoying the winter chill. Joe and I, along with the rest of the *Morning Joe* staff, had just returned from a grueling three-week cross-country trek covering the historic 2008 presidential primaries. It was an exhilarating time to be working on a political talk show.

After months of hard work, *Morning Joe* was becoming the place for candidates to be seen and heard. The buzz was growing, our ratings were improving, and the show was making news. We should have been ecstatic. Instead Joe sat silently and listened as I explained why I needed to resign.

This was a painful decision. But after nearly twenty years of scrambling up, down, and back up the television-news ladder several times over, I was done. I was demoralized—and not because I didn't like my job. In fact, I loved it. No other show I'd ever worked on had such energy and so much excitement. But as I explained to Joe on that sad, cold winter morning, I could no longer work for a network that refused to recognize my value. It may have taken me forty years, but I'd finally realized it was time to do things right . . . or not at all.

Despite my professional experience, the fifteen-hour workdays, and a successful new show that I had helped build, MSNBC was still refusing to pay me what I was worth. Not only was my salary lower than my colleagues', each month was a financial scramble to make ends meet. After child care, on-air wardrobe, makeup, travel, and the other ridiculous expenses that women in this business end up taking on, the job was actually costing me more than I was being paid. Checks were bouncing, and worse, I could barely face myself in the mirror when I thought of the example I was setting for my twelve and fourteen-year-old daughters. Every morning I sat with a group of male colleagues, all of whom made much more than I did. In fact, our salaries weren't even close.

Let me be clear: There is no question that Joe was worth more to the show's success than anyone. But was he really *fourteen* times more valuable than me?

To be fair, Joe and I started out at *Morning Joe* on very different footing. The show was Joe's creation, and his sheer determination got it on the air. He had been hosting his own prime-time talk show at the network, and his salary was on par with that of other prime-time hosts. MSNBC was in the middle of a massive financial restructuring, making difficult staff cuts in an effort to keep the network productive during tough times.

When Joe was pitching me as his cohost, I had been doing a low-level, part-time job at MSNBC, just to get back in the game after losing my anchor position at *CBS Evening News* the year before. I had worked my tail off to help *Morning Joe* become the success it was, and my career was again on the upswing—so really, why was I jeopardizing it? Because I was not getting paid my value. And because, ultimately, I had only myself to blame.

I sat across from Joe over breakfast to tell him that I had reached the breaking point. I owed it to Joe to tell him in person and to thank him for his heroic efforts to revive my career. But the inequity was killing me, and I believed it would ultimately poison the show. I was ready to walk away.

Before I could finish, he said, "No, you can't leave."

Joe knew I wasn't being paid what I was worth and had been fighting for me all along, but so far his efforts had been in vain. He asked for a few more days. As always, Joe had a plan.

The former congressman knew that, as much as anyone, I was responsible for our on-air success. He had told anyone who would listen that his vision for his new show would succeed only if I were his cohost. He was as angry at the NBC brass as I was. But what made matters worse was that I—me, myself—was to blame for this. I had allowed this to happen. I had asked repeatedly for a raise, but I had repeatedly been denied. The truth is, like most women, I didn't know my value, and even if I had, I wouldn't have known how to get it.

Looking back, I realize that every time I sat at the negotiating table, my greatest enemy was myself. The words I chose and the strategies I put in play actually undermined my goals. No manager and no network executive was responsible for my plight. The failure to effectively communicate rested solely on me—every time.

My meeting with Joe that February morning was the culmination of a problem that had been brewing for decades. I had spent my career moving from job to job, accepting pay that I knew wasn't competitive because I always felt lucky to be there. I figured that if I just worked hard, took on more hours, more assignments, and more stories, I could prove myself, and eventually my bosses would reward me with a raise and promotion. Often while I was hustling and hoping for more money, I would discover that my male colleagues were making more than I was. I wouldn't get angry at the men for this—I'd be angry at myself for not earning more respect (and compensation) from management. Then I'd start feeling underappreciated, talk to other networks, and then move on and repeat the pattern somewhere else. Clearly the pattern wasn't getting me anywhere.

Why was I continually underpaid and undervalued? Was it because I was a woman? No. There are women in this business who rake in huge salaries. Like me, they are commodities. But these women know their value, and they get it. So what were they doing that I wasn't?

I had spent months watching Joe get what he wanted from management with ease and determination. I, too, was capable of doing great things for the show, but when it came to fighting for myself, I always struck out. I began asking myself whether I was the biggest idiot on the face of the earth. Here I was, playing the role of a strong, successful woman on the set who takes on the political hotshots and keeps the guys in check. And yet my salary was where it might have been fifteen years ago, or even twenty years ago. This wasn't where I should have been at my age and level of experience.

I started to think about what was keeping me back, and what was keeping all women back. I kept seeing headlines about how far women have come. They have broken glass ceilings. Almost ten years later, Hillary Clinton has run for president, twice. During her second run, she won the popular vote. And yet women's salaries still don't equal men's salaries—women everywhere still make less.

I thought to myself, "Is it possible? Is it possible that I'm not alone? Have other successful women had some of the same problems? Or am I alone?" I started talking to the incredibly impressive women on the set, and they all told me, "Oh, no, no. You're not alone." One of these women actually came to me for advice when she was changing jobs, and I realized she was doing the same thing. Undermining herself. Undercutting herself. Undervaluing herself.

Ultimately, MSNBC showed me the money. I got a significant raise, but not in the way I would ever have anticipated. Mine truly was an unconventional path, and I advise you not to walk it yourself. I'll tell you more about my experience later in the book.

To its credit, MSNBC not only made good, but it has taken up the cause. After I got this book contract I went to our boss, Phil Griffin—one of the stars in this book and the man who passed on giving me a raise until I was able to effectively communicate my value. I said to him, "Listen, I've got a book deal. I'm going to write about knowing my value, and I'm going to write about the mistakes I've made. And I want to write about mistakes I've made with you." He thought about it for less than a second and said, "Absolutely."

Even after reading the manuscript of this book, Phil has been on board as my biggest cheerleader. He knows a story that will resonate and, yes, sell. He was also just as happy to interview for the expanded edition as he was for the original manuscript; he has maintained the belief, even after all these years, that this message is important and needs to be shared to both NBC employees and beyond. But all of this came as a result of years of mistakes on my part, and hopefully, like me, you can learn from them.

Rebuilding My Career, but Not My Value

When I started at MSNBC in 2007, I was really starting over.

At the time, I had been out of work for almost a year after losing my job as a weekend anchor and a *60 Minutes* contributor at CBS News. In the wake of a scandal about a *60 Minutes* story on George Bush's military record and a management shake-up, I was let go with hardly any notice and little financial cushion.

I spent the year that followed searching for a job with the help of an agent who arranged meetings for me with executives at the various broadcast and cable networks. Every month, my prospects went down a rung. First, my agent was able to set up meetings with network presidents. Then I was meeting with vice presidents, then talent recruiters. Before long, I could barely get an appointment with anyone. I was nearly forty years old, and my career was in shambles—basically I was old news. My best days appeared to be behind me, and I wasn't considered a worthwhile investment.

After months of fruitless searching, I realized the right strategy was to start over. I had worked at NBC's cable division earlier in my career, and I liked it there. The people knew me, and it had been a good fit. So I called MSNBC and begged for a job. Not a job they thought I would take given my experience, not a job they thought I would want, but whatever on-air job they had available. Reluctantly, the president of NBC News told me there was an opening for a newsreader position: someone who would read thirty-second news updates, called cut-ins, three times a night on MSNBC. He was describing a low-paying freelance position, and I grabbed onto it for dear life, like a ledge that I hoped would stop the freefall of my career.

If you looked at that MSNBC job in the context of my resume, you'd see that it was a considerable step back from my high-profile correspondent job at CBS. The position was even a big step back from my job at MSNBC ten years earlier. I spent my fortieth birthday doing cut-ins, but it was fine. It was work, and I was proud of myself. My girls were watching Mommy take a huge step back in order to bring home a paycheck. There was as much value in this moment as the day I got a huge contract at CBS that included a *60 Minutes* deal. I was going to be okay. We were going to be okay.

After a year of having their mother home and with money being tight, my two daughters were ready for me to go back to work. They were used to me as a working mom, and they knew I enjoyed it. Work was what made me sparkle, and it was what I contributed to the household.

I earned money far better than I cooked dinner. The job reading news cut-ins would be a piece of cake, and a part-time position was better than no position. I had to be realistic about my current value in the marketplace.

While I have regrets about not knowing what my compensation could and should have been at key moments in my career, I look back at the decision to take that job with great pride. Part of knowing your value is knowing when it is down, and knowing when it's time to rebuild. My biggest challenge has been knowing when my stock is up.

My first months back at MSNBC, I worked about four hours each day. In between my thirty-second news cut-ins, I paid my bills and listened over the phone to my girls' piano practice. After a year of unemployment, this job was just fine. The work was predictable, it was good for the kids, and it was great to be back in the game . . . but the work was boring. Extremely boring. I felt confident of my talent, but I couldn't do much with it in that position.

It wasn't long before the executive producer of daytime-news programming recruited me to substitute-host full news hours during the day. Within weeks I was on the schedule for the cut-ins as well as the full hour at three PM on weekdays. MSNBC and NBC started to give me assignments throughout the building, and my days became more interesting and a lot longer with no increase in my day rate. All over again, I had to show my value for free.

My hosting duties weren't as high-profile as the role I had played at MSNBC seven years earlier when I cohosted the women's show *Home-Page* with Ashleigh Banfield and Gina Gaston. Nor was it on the level of my lead role covering the 2000 presidential election and recount. But it was a job in the field I love. I was glad to be working again and realized it was a huge step back. My stock was down. I had to rebuild, and it was frustrating. At times, it was also ridiculous.

After my first time substitute-hosting an hour of news, the word spread quickly about my performance; my new colleagues, who remembered nothing of my long history in the business, were coming up to me in the halls, giving me high-fives and saying, "Wow! You're really good!" I often joke about the fact that men are really good at "pressing reset" (one of the key tenets of knowing your value), because they remember absolutely nothing. A male executive producer who I worked with the last time I was an extremely competent full host at MSNBC was literally walking around saying, "Wow, we should give that Mika Brzezinski a second look, she's pretty damn good!!!"

Insert my best Marge Simpson imitation here: "Mmmmmmmhph." That's the sound she makes when Homer says something so painfully obvious, she just has no words.

In this business, you are as good as your last story. On cable, apparently you are as good as your last on-air minute. The same thing happened when I was tapped to do an NBC News Special Report when Brian Williams was unavailable and no one else was around. My delivery was flawless (of course), and once again, everyone seemed so surprised. No one remembered or had any idea that I had done dozens of special reports for CBS News. So here I was, suddenly an up-and-comer all over again. At forty.

Still, I smiled and accepted the compliments. I was grateful for the opportunity to show the producers what I could do. The network realized I was useful, and I was convinced that sooner or later the right job would open up for me. Three months later, it did.

In May 2007, Don Imus was pulled off the air for making offensive statements about the Rutgers University women's basketball players during his early-morning show. Immediately there was a three-hour void on the MSNBC airwaves. I remember thinking, "Oh god, I hope they don't make me fill those hours reading news—what a miserable shift."

Little did I know how many high-profile male television personalities were maneuvering for the spot. Filling Imus's shoes was a very big deal.

A few days after the Imus firing, I bumped into Joe Scarborough, an MSNBC prime-time talk show host and former Florida congressman. Joe worked out of a studio in Pensacola, Florida, and he was in town to audition for the Imus slot. I had never met him. I knew his face only because when I read my daily news cut-ins, I would do what's called a toss-back to his news and opinion show, *Scarborough Country*, and he would pop up on the monitors in front of me. Every night at 7:59, I'd say, "That's a look at the news. Now back to *Scarborough Country*." I never watched the show because I was always yanking off my microphone and hurrying back to find new ways to fill my downtime.

Joe introduced himself, and after a brief conversation I could see wheels turning in his head. He asked me if I would be interested in hosting the morning show with him. My answer was, "Why?" His question didn't make any sense. I told him I was a forty-year-old washed-up newswoman and housewife from Westchester. His response was, "Exactly! Someone real!" He was dead serious. I was thrown off, because I was serious, too: I knew what television executives were looking for, and it wasn't me. But Joe seemed to recognize the contribution I could make to the show. I liked that. He seemed to want me as myself, rather than someone acting the part of a television cohost. If he meant what he said, it would be an intriguing opportunity.

Still, I was reticent about signing on to an early-morning show, which would throw my household into disarray. My family had put up with my crazy nights and early-morning shifts many times as I was scrambling up the career ladder, and they had picked me up after it collapsed beneath me. Why would I put them through that again? Why would I want to put myself through it again? Did I need a demanding job in television, or did I need a predictable one? After all I'd been through, I realized I was kind of happy with the predictable, and I was reluctant to put everything on the line again.

But Joe is nothing if not persuasive. He was hyperfocused on his concept for a groundbreaking political talk show. There would be no rehearsal and no script, just a cast of sharp journalists and analysts, all handpicked by him, who could engage in lively and intelligent discussions while treating one another with respect. He wanted real conversation, long interviews, and true reactions. He was determined to make his vision of the show a reality. He knew what would work, and what would work was for me to be his cohost.

My gut told me that he was gifted. That he had a really good idea, and that his idea was going to change the way news was delivered on television. Joe's concepts seemed exciting and innovative to me as a woman who had spent two decades in an industry that did little more than rehash tired news formats. This show would be a wild ride, and Joe was inviting me along.

I didn't really know what I was stepping into on that first day back in 2007. But within seconds of being on the air together, I knew I was a part of something unique. I was not aware that we would ultimately turn out to be a couple, which was truly unique on a news program. I simply knew that this was good TV, and good TV is hard to come by.

That morning, I was on the set at 5:55 AM. Joe and I began discussing the latest political news before the cameras started rolling, and we just kept talking as the program went live. "Five, four, three, two, one . . ." We just kept talking. In a random trick of fate, we had immediate on-air chemistry. We had only met the day before, but you would have thought we had been at this for years. Later in the day, my best friend called me and asked, "How long have you known that guy?" She was astonished when I said I just met him yesterday.

I have been on my share of new shows; you can tell very quickly if something works or not. Most are duds. I knew immediately that *Morning Joe* would be a hit. Much TV is conventional and safe; each show gets tied up with a neat little bow at the end. But this show was different. It was unpredictable and risky, and extremely smart. Both Joe and I had been beaten up in our respective careers, and that experience—plus the fact that we were both bored by the traditional television news format—made us fearless. And we were. I thought to myself, "This is the kind of breakthrough show I'd want my girls to see me host. I like watching this, and I like doing this."

When we heard we'd won the Imus slot, we were off and running.

From that moment, our team began working around the clock to build *Morning Joe* into the success it is today. We had a tiny staff and limited resources, but we had big plans and even more determination. We didn't engage in shrill dialogue to win ratings or deliver packaged reports that were safe and pat. We told the truth as we saw it. We said what we thought, and sometimes we were wrong. We were ourselves, come what may, and people responded immediately. Everyone knew that we all cared to be there despite our differences, and we all genuinely liked one another.

Ours would become the show that the *New York Times* described as "unlike anything else on morning television," that the *New Yorker* called "appallingly entertaining," and that *Forbes* magazine proclaimed "the hottest morning show around." But it would take a Herculean effort to get there.

Joe was the creator. I was the executor. He focused on ideas and pushed them through the MSNBC hierarchy. He fought for my job, our producer Chris Licht's job, and other on- and off-air people whom he felt were the right fit. Building the team took up most of his day after we got off the air. He brought on Willie Geist as the bright young personality who would add youth and attitude. My job was to bring in the big-name newsmakers to our brand-new, and at that point unknown, very-early-morning show. I took my BlackBerry (yes, a BlackBerry!) everywhere and worked it around the clock.

I used all the skills I had developed from years of chasing stories as a reporter. I worked every angle, every connection. I got up at three AM every day, but if I needed to call a contact at eight PM, I pushed myself to sound perky and awake. Aggressive. On a mission. I kept the phone at my ear while I jogged. Joe and Chris and I would have strategy sessions as I thumped along my four-mile route, panting, sweating, and thinking, "How can we make the show better?"

The three of us realized we had stumbled onto a rare opportunity in the odd and unpredictable world of TV news and "opinion television." We had been given a three-hour window over which we had complete control. MSNBC was still busy dealing with the fallout from the Imus situation, and as with many new shows, the network simply let ours fly to see how it did on its own.

I have to hand it to MSNBC president Phil Griffin. He knew we were on to something and that we needed space to work out the kinks. Only a confident, sharp manager would have had that foresight. There are not many of his kind in television news: He fought for us and protected us from unnecessary tweaking from upstairs.

Before long, *Morning Joe*'s future was looking bright, but mine still wasn't. The network brass weren't convinced that I was the right cohost. They gave me a new contract and moved me from freelance into a staff position, but the money was barely better, and I was not formally assigned to *Morning Joe*. That meant I had to be available to work for any—and every—other show that needed me. My days began with a four AM commute into New Jersey, where I would trudge up to the makeup room and have my face painted; most days I didn't scrape that makeup off for sixteen hours. Often I would be on the air four or five hours a day, then spend the rest of my waking hours chasing guests for the next day's *Morning Joe* and doing any other jobs that MSNBC assigned. I didn't want to seem difficult by turning down extra assignments. I figured if management was asking me to take on more, that meant they had actually considered my workload and felt I should be able to handle additional tasks.

The ink on my new contract was barely dry when I realized my mistake.

Joe and I worked so closely as we put this show together that we pretty much knew everything about each other. He'd answer my phone and talk to my kids, and I'd answer his phone and talk to his. Phil called, or Joe's agent called, and they'd negotiate a detail in his latest contract, and I'd be sitting right there listening. So I knew there was a vast difference in our salaries. We talked openly about the money he was getting and the money that I should be getting. He was very concerned and hoped that I would be a permanent part of the show, and I think we were both just relieved when I finally had a contract in hand.

The reality of my situation began to dawn on me when I learned that Willie Geist had just re-signed as well, but his was a contract to be on the show, whereas mine was simply to be on MSNBC. Someone had said, "Just sign this," and I signed a generic contract that had me working on any shift, including *Morning Joe*, but without the title "*Morning Joe* cohost." It said MSNBC could also ask me to do *Nightly News* pieces, *Weekend Today* news reading, and hours and hours filling in for other anchors in the afternoon. Willie was smarter about the negotiation and cut himself a better deal. He asked for what he wanted, and he didn't show up to work until he got it. When I heard through the grapevine that he was making more than I was, I realized I had done myself a great disservice. I didn't value myself, and I had taken a deal that reflected that.

I was stunned to learn that Willie made more, but I was happy for him. I've always known he's a great talent, and I'm sure his value will explode in the coming years. I'm good at predicting these things for other people.*

I JUST COULDN'T BELIEVE how stupid I'd been on my own behalf, how my own sense of value was so deflated by low self-esteem and a misplaced sense of gratitude. I was demoralized, but I was determined to show up shining every morning. Balancing the job, the family, and the hours was exhausting, but knowing that what appeared to be a career high was really a complete failure was truly depressing.

Living with that reality was bringing out an emotion in me that does not work for a woman in the workplace, at least not mine: anger. *Morning Joe* shows me at my best and my worst. Our show is transparent and real. We hide nothing. It all shows: the effects of exhaustion (and Ambien), all our moods and emotions. I knew anger wouldn't rate. I would have to find a way to be happy, or at least at peace.

I had taken a tremendous risk in accepting this job. I didn't have financial security, and my career was hanging in the balance. On top of

---

*As I write this expanded edition, I am astounded at just how right this sentence was when I first wrote it. Look at Willie today. If I might say so myself, I was spot on. Willie's career has exploded. When his last contract was up, every network wanted him. He landed an amazing opportunity with *Sunday Today*—counter to CBS *Sunday Morning* where his dad is a legend. But while Joe and I have always been good at recognizing talent, I can see now that the only person whose talent I didn't value was my own.

that, I was working with a man who refused to follow a conventional path. Some called him a rule breaker. But I knew he was actually a game changer.

That same rebellious streak that ruffled feathers in Congress made Joe a controversial figure in the halls of NBC. While everybody else played it safe, Joe demanded that we push the envelope. Needless to say, that earned me few new friends at 30 Rock. Many tried to talk me out of working with him, even offering me the "safety" of a slot on another "more legitimate" broadcast. But I refused to listen to them. I went in a different direction, and I'm extremely proud of that fact. I don't know any women who would have done what I did in that instance. I went my own way, ripped up my own script. That takes experience and self-knowledge. The ability to be brave, to try something new, to take a risk, to know it's good when it's good—that's worth something. And if you're going to take a major risk, you sure as hell better know what it's worth. I can do that. I'm proud because accepting the cohost job meant accepting so much risk. And so much fighting. And so much standing up in the face of rejection. And so much pushback from NBC management and my new bosses, who I instinctively wanted to please.

But I was still clueless when it came to translating that powerful sense of self-worth into actual dollars and cents.

Despite the money, I didn't think of leaving. I was invested in *Morning Joe* and engrossed in the story we were covering: the 2008 race for the White House. The combination of the first African-American major-party nominee and the lightning speed of the news cycle in the age of social media made the 2008 presidential race unlike any other election I had covered.

Instead of walking away from MSNBC when I first realized I was underpaid, I worked harder to get the candidates booked on our show. It helped that my brother Ian worked for John McCain; my father, former national security advisor to President Carter, had endorsed Obama early on; and my other brother, Mark, worked for President Clinton and was joining the Obama organization to help out. If I didn't know someone at a campaign, I'd bluff my way in until I got to know someone. Before long, I had lined up interviews with every candidate from Barack Obama to Ron Paul.

Joe and I knew that this election was our opportunity to really put *Morning Joe* on the map. No one was going to do it for us. We would do everything for ourselves. Other morning shows had a staff of forty to fifty people and the full support of being "management's choice"; we had a staff of eight, our BlackBerrys, and the belief that we could do it. We knew we had to be scrappy and relentless. So we ran around the country, basically carrying the show on our backs, and working around the clock to make it must-see political TV.

There was no better example of how alone we were at times than the Iowa caucuses. We wanted to take *Morning Joe* to Iowa, but MSNBC wasn't sold on it enough at that point to spend the money. Management liked us, just not that much. We knew we had to be on the ground in Iowa. We fought and fought, and still hit brick walls. They told us there was not enough room in the budget and not enough room in the convention center, where all the other networks had built their sets.

Joe, Chris, and I refused to take no for an answer. We forged ahead. I kept calling all the campaigns and asking them to stop by our studio set—a set that did not yet exist in the minds of MSNBC management. Chris worked on the travel and producing details as if we were going. On the eve of New Year's weekend, Joe called Phil Griffin and laid down the law. "Phil, we are going to Iowa," he said. "If you want us on the air on Monday, you might want to send a few cameras. If you don't, you will have shots of empty chairs in New York. Your call, but we are going to Iowa."

MSNBC finally gave Phil the money, and within forty-eight hours we were scrambling to kiss our families good-bye and make our flights. Joe flew from Florida and made it there first. But Chris and I got stuck in Chicago because of storms and air-traffic delays. We had ten hours to make it to Des Moines, 300 miles away. Chris and I grabbed a rental car—without my luggage, because it was lost. We drove all night through a blizzard to make our five AM Des Moines broadcast. We arrived several hours before airtime. I was so worn down, I even ate McDonald's chicken nuggets and fries for breakfast; as someone who aspires to be a paragon of healthy living, that was a desperate act.

With no room for a *Morning Joe* set at the convention center, we set up a makeshift studio at Java Joe's, a popular Des Moines coffee shop filled with locals. Soon, every candidate showed up at Java Joe's and stayed a while to drink coffee and shoot the breeze. The result was spontaneous and spirited conversations that engrossed viewers and participants alike. I was running on no sleep but made it through five hours of programming that morning. After seeing the first hour of the show—the show no one wanted to send to Iowa—Phil got so excited that he asked us to stay on the air two extra hours. MSNBC's front-office would later tell us those five hours were among the network's best hours of campaign coverage.

It was at Java Joe's that we received the blessing from the king of political news, NBC News's Washington bureau chief and moderator of *Meet the Press*, Tim Russert. He was over at the convention center doing the *Today Show*, but it was clear to Tim that the excitement in Iowa was at Java Joe's. When the door swung open and Tim walked in saying, "Hey, you guys mind if I get on the show?" we were thrilled. He stayed on for an hour and then hung out in the background for the rest of the morning talking to candidates and campaign managers. The whole morning flew by and felt like magic.

Phil Griffin had already given us some unforgettable advice: "You all should look at it this way: You have an audience of one. You need to ask yourself, 'Would Tim like this?'" So when Tim, the head of the network's political coverage, joined us at the center of the action, it was as if we'd received a true royal blessing. We believe Tim's support and presence helped set the path for our future. He passed away in June of 2008, but we will never forget what he did for us. We will never forget our audience of one.

Phil called Joe during the broadcast the second day. "Hey, can you do this in New Hampshire too?" he asked. "And what about Michigan and South Carolina?"

All our hard work was paying off. Our ratings soared. MSNBC was keeping us on the air an extra three hours every day, six in total. *Morning Joe* had quickly become the place for presidential candidates to be seen and heard. It was the show of choice for political junkies and viewers tired of the standard morning broadcast fare. Our audience was growing, and the show itself was making news.

While we were on the road, I tried to push my salary concerns aside. I didn't want to deal with the situation; I certainly didn't have time. Yet the money issue kept surfacing. At times when I should have been celebrating, I grew morose and discouraged.

Playing the Victim: Mistake Number One

Three months into *Morning Joe*'s run, I started getting e-mails making fun of my clothes. One day I wore a vivid pattern, and a viewer wrote, "What painter threw up on Mika?"

Part of my job is to look fresh sitting among a bunch of men at six AM. In a visual medium, appearances matter. Clothes are part of the production element of a talk show. If not handled correctly, they become a distraction that interferes with the substance of the broadcast. That said, nobody cares what the men wear or how they style their hair. Joe rolls out of bed at 5:45 AM and jumps in the car to make the top of the show with only seconds to spare, his face still puffy and creased from sleep. He'll take his seat wearing a fleece sweater and run his hand through his hair to brush it. If he were a woman, he would be called a disgrace.

Being a woman over forty on TV requires that I wake up around 3:30 every morning and go through a numbing routine in order to look presentable on high-definition TV. A female anchor's hair, makeup, and clothes are scrutinized both inside and outside the network, and if something seems off, she will hear about it in e-mails or even a phone call from the front office.

NBC wasn't providing a wardrobe, so I had to fend for myself on *Morning Joe*. I found out very quickly that it was extremely difficult for me to handle the clothing aspect of being on the air three hours a day. I didn't need Chanel or Gucci, but I needed to look put together and, at the very least, make sure my clothes and hair were not a distraction. But looking camera-ready requires a wardrobe, and assembling a wardrobe takes a lot of time and costs a lot of money—the two things in my life that were in short supply.

I remember one time running down to the Lord & Taylor near my home and grabbing a bunch of cheap V-neck sweaters. I figured I would save time searching for "new" outfits by simply wearing different colors.

A few weeks later, those sweaters wore out their welcome. I began receiving rude comments via e-mail about wearing the same thing every day. Some of these messages came from determined viewers who managed to find their way into my personal inbox. If a handful of viewers felt so strongly that they'd try that hard to get through to me, they probably weren't alone.

Clothes and hair were becoming my daily enemy. They represented everything that was wrong with my position at MSNBC. Not only was I was not getting paid what I was worth, but after the added cost of a new wardrobe and quality haircuts, I was actually losing money by working at the network.

I knew I deserved a raise. I knew I needed a raise. But I still felt anxious about asking to be compensated for what I was bringing to the show. Lots of people considered me a hit, but how did I really know that management agreed? My current salary implied that they still thought of me as a freelancer.

I brought all these feelings with me when I asked for a raise. I actually thought that if I explained to NBC's front office about the clothes and the travel, and how the math didn't make sense, they would respond to my concerns. Looking back (and knowing what I've learned while writing this book), I may as well have said, "Hi. Please don't give me a raise, okay?"

I went to see Phil Griffin, who to this day is a friend, but we didn't know each other that well then. I sat down in his office and said, "I'm sorry if this is bad timing. I don't want to be a problem. I'm absolutely certain that this is a great show. I'm buying clothes for the shift, I'm buying makeup, I'm trying to keep my hair the way it should look." I went on to say, "I really don't want to be a diva or high maintenance or anything. But the way the numbers add up at the end of the month, I need to make more. I really hope you can understand that."

I was nervous and struggling to articulate both facts and emotions. I was appealing to what I thought would be his . . . what, generous side? It certainly wasn't Phil's job to care about wardrobe details, and I had signed an agreement. The conversation was a disaster. Needless to say, I left Phil's office without a raise, but it would be unfair to focus the blame on him. At that time, I still didn't realize why my plea failed. I didn't know what was wrong with my approach, and given my age and professional experience, that's simply not right.

By the time we returned to New York from covering the primaries, the tension was building. We were still working like hell, moving on to Election Day and the inauguration. Work was a constant, driving battle. Every day I could feel myself edging one step closer to the breaking point. I was doing four long hours, and the guys were lumbering off the set at nine, going to relax in their offices. I'd continue to book the show, and push the show, and travel for the show into the night. Every day I grew tenser and tenser; again, it was nobody's fault but my own. I knew there was really no point in blaming Joe or Willie. I liked them, and they deserved everything they were getting and more. They were smart enough to get it. That was clear with every meeting that we had with management and every phone call that I overheard. The men around me were doing a good job of getting what they wanted and deserved. The inequity became tougher to overlook.

I was angry at myself, and certainly my family was paying the price at home all over again. I'd gone from unemployed to finding a free-lance job that was totally doable and a good transition for them, to quite frankly working harder than I ever did at *60 Minutes*, which really seemed like the ultimate in exhausting, hard-driving, competitive, tough, constantly explosive, stressful work. But this was even more intense and all-consuming.

Joe was growing more furious by the day. He had believed in me from the start, and he wanted me to focus solely on *Morning Joe*. He probably saw me getting in my own way as I tried to get my due, but being aware of the challenges all women in television face, he knew how difficult it would be for me to solve this problem on my own. It never occurred to me during this time that it was my job to just say no. Many days I was exhausted and depressed. I would tell myself if I worked harder, I'd prove my worth and eventually the bosses would notice and reward me. It would be a fruitless wait on my part—and self-destructive.

I had minimized my own value to my boss by whining about clothing costs, when the real reason that I deserved a raise would have made a much more compelling argument. Hemming and hawing about expenses was so unbelievably below the level I had achieved. The fact was, I had been busting my ass, and the show would be nothing without me. I was a critical component of the rapidly developing *Morning Joe* brand.

When your stock is up, you need to walk in there knowing it. I am shocked to this day at how blind I was to the reality of my own value, and how destructive playing the victim was to my negotiation. Everything was so personally insulting. I sweated the small stuff and then let them see me sweat. Total Know Your Value system failure. Never take an insulting business offer personally. Be smarter. Rise above the petty issues so you can see the value of your contributions from 20,000 feet. Only then can you advocate for yourself effectively.

CHAPTER 2

GET OUT OF YOUR WAY

Women as Their Own Worst Enemies

My story, with Valerie Jarrett, Tina Brown, Carol Smith,
Sheryl Sandberg, Carol Bartz, Lesley Jane Seymour,
Nora Ephron, Arianna Huffington, and Suze Orman

The Paris Hilton Incident

Despite the network's misgivings, Joe and I knew that our partnership on the air was driving the show's appeal. In fact, just one month into our run, our chemistry would put *Morning Joe* on the map.

The show's fans know it as "the Paris Hilton incident." The story began the morning socialite Paris Hilton, released from prison after serving minimal time for violating probation, walked through a blinding gauntlet of frenzied photographers. Her release was written as the lead for our news-headlines segment on a day when the Iraq war should have been at the head. I couldn't believe this junk was being passed off as news, so Joe and I called it out by mocking ourselves and the news business as a whole. At first I held up the news script and simply announced I wouldn't read it; then Joe goaded me into ripping, burning, and shredding it at the top of each hour of our three-hour show.

The episode was emblematic of what makes the *Morning Joe* chemistry work: our ability to act instinctively and say what we think without fear. We call each other out. We call other journalists out. We call politicians out. We do it with humor and transparency, and we do it with the credibility of having been there: we're guided by our collective experience in the fields of politics and news. Our life lessons have taught us many things, including not taking ourselves too seriously.

Ripping up the script was an unremarkable act to the *Morning Joe* team, but we discovered that in the world of 24/7 news, it was a minor-league sensation. For some reason, the Paris Hilton incident hit a nerve. Someone posted the video clip on YouTube and it went viral, seen by millions of viewers around the world. The incident helped introduce *Morning Joe* to a whole new set of viewers. To this day, I am applauded and thanked by rabid news junkies who say they will never forget that moment. I am amazed that ten years later, people still bring it up. They tell us repeatedly that our show is refreshing because all the players are candid about their beliefs and biases, which apparently is something viewers have been looking for.

Was my value suddenly changing? Could it be that what looked like "forty and washed-up" was now "experienced and gutsy"? Joe had assured me of that every step of the way. But I was programmed differently. I had my doubts. Looking back, I simply could not see that my stock was up. Women are way too good at knowing when they are not flourishing. We are the first to point out our weaknesses. But when we nail it, we have no sense that this is a moment not to be wasted. This is a moment to pounce, to cash in, to do what men do—toot our own horn!

The day after the Paris Hilton incident, a top NBC executive—a woman—called me into her office and asked me to take a seat. Her stern expression told me that this was not a victory lap. She was clearly unhappy that I had ripped up the Paris Hilton script. In a sharp tone she warned me that I would now have a reputation for being a "problem" and "difficult." She was "concerned" that people "wouldn't like" me. Yes, this happened. My gut said she was nuts and wrong. But my mouth did something different.

I apologized.

I stammered about why it happened, and was about to assure her that it would not happen again.

As she paced her office looking like she was about to fire me, her assistant barged in with an urgent call. She left the room. I sat there alone, wondering whether I had apologized enough.

Five minutes later, the executive returned. I don't know who had been on the other end of that urgent call or what was said, but her tone and body language had done a sudden 180. "We want to offer you your own show," she said brightly, "at nine AM, after *Morning Joe*. A full hour. All yours. You get to cohost *Morning Joe*, and then you get to host your own show. All yours!"

I must have had a slight case of whiplash. Clearly I wasn't thinking straight, because what did I do next?

(Today's Mika would have whispered in the Mika of 2008's ear "Ummmmm . . . hello? Mika?? An opportunity to get more money! Right here, right now. You see it, right???" No. No, I did not.)

I thanked her.

Seriously. And I left, relieved I wasn't in trouble.

(Today's Mika is closing her laptop and smashing it against her forehead three times. This stuff is painful to relive! WHY CAN'T A WOMAN SEE WHEN HER STOCK IS UP? Okay, laptop back open.)

My success on *Morning Joe* meant that I would now be responsible for another hour of television every day. While it may look casual and spontaneous, hosting *Morning Joe*, a political show with no tele-prompter or safety net, is incredibly demanding work. Its success depends on my instincts, my up-to-the-minute knowledge of world events, and my mind being clear so that I can ad-lib no matter the situation. Three hours of extemporaneous discussion and debate were considered a hard slog for any television host or anchor.

As I looked around the table on the *Morning Joe* set the next day, I realized what I had done. Joe and Willie stretched and yawned at the end of our three hours and talked about how tired they were and how our schedule was insane. Then they wandered off the set to finally collapse somewhere. I was just getting started on the additional full hour, an hour I would now have to fill every day. By myself. I was still the lowest-paid on the set despite four hours each day on the air. No other anchor on television worked those hours five days a week. At the end of every *Morning Joe*, at 8:55 Eastern Time, we have a short segment where we all take a turn saying what we've learned that day. That morning I should have said, "I learned that I am an ass." How could I have missed this opportunity to ask for what I deserved?

The moment I was offered the extra hour—five minutes after being admonished for "misbehavior"—I should have gotten up and left without responding to the proposal. I should have been saddened and shocked by the way she treated me. I should have told her I needed to think twice about whether I wanted to work at an organization that didn't value my instincts. I had the moment right there! I should have milked it! (Today's Mika is now banging her head against her kitchen table!) Clearly the ratings, e-mails, and calls to NBC were telling execs that I was a rock star of the news biz. I threw away all that leverage, because I didn't "get it" in real time. Why don't women see their value . . . in the moment?

But as I started talking to women—especially researchers—I heard many stories and statistics that surprised me. The simple fact is that women don't ask for raises as often as men do. My problem wasn't just a personal failing, it was a common experience. We don't recognize and jump on the opportunity to strike while the iron is hot.

IN THE FIRST of many conversations with successful women, I sat down with former Obama senior advisor Valerie Jarrett and shared my story. She listened and nodded all-too-knowingly.

"We are our own worst enemy," Jarrett says, understanding exactly how I had been tripped up. "Somehow it's unseemly for women to promote themselves. We think that there's a meritocracy that's hierarchical, and the people at the top make the decisions about what promotions are based on."

As a female and an African-American, Jarrett says she always expected to face obstacles in the workplace: "My parents raised me to think because I was a girl and because I was black I was going to have to work twice as hard. They did it with no chip on their shoulder—it was just a fact of life, get used to it. Don't try to change what is, just work twice as hard."

So she says that's what she did. She worked hard and kept her head down. But Jarrett didn't expect that working hard would not automatically lead to advancement and better pay.

> *I felt that if I was deserving,*
> *then my boss should recognize that*
> *I was deserving.* —VALERIE JARRETT

"I kept doing more and more work," Jarrett tells me. She describes an experience she had when she worked in the real estate division of the City of Chicago's Department of Law early in her career. Jarrett felt fortunate to have the job, but she wasn't advancing. She says she was lucky to have a female mentor, Lucille Dobbins, who instructed her: "Lucille said to me, 'You are doing more work than your supervisor and your supervisor's supervisor . . . you should be a deputy.' I said, 'Well, my boss knows I'm working hard, and he values what I'm doing.' She said, 'You can't sit around waiting for people to recognize your work, you have to ask for it. You need to go in there and tell him you should be a deputy. And you should tell him you want to be in the front suite of offices, because he doesn't have a woman in the front suite.'"

"Did that seem weird to you?" I ask.

"It seemed like absolutely horrible advice," Jarrett answers. "I thought [my boss] would humiliate me and tell me to get out of his office."

Still, Jarrett gathered her courage and went for it. "I said, 'This is the work I'm doing, this is the level of complexity, and I really think I should be a deputy,'" she tells me. "He looked at me and said, 'Okay.'"

Jarrett was shocked. She got the promotion and the front office. "I felt that if I was deserving, then my boss should recognize that I was deserving," she reasons. "That's what bosses do."

Jarrett says her mentor taught her an important lesson: "What Lucille brought to my attention was that I was not valuing my own work and that I needed to be my own best advocate. And that is something that women seldom do and men do intuitively. Men ask for it all the time. Women never do. Women expect that if you do really well, someone will recognize your performance and will reward you accordingly."

While this seems obvious, for many women—even a top presidential advisor—simply asking can be difficult. Jarrett says that asking for that promotion "was one of the most uncomfortable conversations that I have ever had."

If you're not asking for a promotion . . . you're not going to get the gold ring. —VALERIE JARRETT

Jarrett says that while we women sit around waiting, men are busy charging the hill. "If you're number four, five, or six, and there's a guy who's four, five, or six, he's going to ask to be number one," she points out. "If you're not asking for a promotion and you're waiting for your merit to be recognized, men are going to hire you to be close, but you're not going to get the gold ring."

Tina Brown—journalist, author, cofounder of *The Daily Beast*, regular on *Morning Joe*, former editor-in-chief of *Newsweek* (the first woman to hold the position in the magazine's seventy-eight-year history), and founder and CEO of Tina Brown Live Media—told me a similar story, but from the perspective of a boss.

Brown is a friend and mentor, and a regular on the show. Our lives are a constant swirl, and in order to get a few moments to talk about the subject of women and compensation, we had to seize the moment. I ended up sitting down with her in a cold dressing room in between segments on *Morning Joe*. She had her coat on, ready to run to the airport and catch a flight, but she took the time to think aloud on this issue and share her valuable perspective.

"I was in a situation, within *The Daily Beast*, where I realized I had overlooked a woman who had been doing a fantastic job. We had brought a man in to do the job, and he failed, horribly. And then we hired another person, who came in and failed. Finally the woman came to see someone at the company and said, 'Look, I've sat here, and I've seen two guys fail at this job. What about me?'"

Brown was astonished that she'd overlooked this person once, let alone twice: "I said to my executive editor, 'You know, this is terrible. The first time someone failed, we should have gone to her . . . she's clearly so much better.'" Brown says that she was ashamed she hadn't recognized the female employee's value in the first place. But, that said, the employee hadn't stepped up and asked for the work.

Brown wasn't the only female manager who admitted to making that same mistake. Women employees just don't seem to have the confidence to raise their hand, to put it out there, to say "Hey! I'm worth this!" So they're overlooked by female bosses and male bosses alike.

We women think we will work very, very hard . . .
and then the money will come. —CAROL SMITH

After an extensive career at Time Warner and nearly a decade as the chief brand officer at *Elle*, Carol Smith has employed thousands of women during her years of overseeing women's magazines. She admits she sees women like me all the time: "We women think we will work very, very hard—we will work harder than anybody in the office—we will get the gold star, and then the money will come. When the money doesn't come, instead of walking into the boss's office and saying, 'I've done this, I've done this, I've done this, and now I need this,' we sit around and earn one-fifteenth of what the man next door earns.

"I think what we have to do is recognize that if we don't ask, it's not coming our way. Men ask all the time; it's not that [the money] just comes to them. I swear it doesn't," Smith says.

Why don't we ask? That's a good question.

Linda Babcock, a professor of economics at Carnegie Mellon University and researcher on the subject of women and negotiation, co-wrote a fascinating book called *Women Don't Ask*. Babcock says women ask for raises and promotions 85 percent less often than their male counterparts. And when women do ask, on average they ask for 30 percent less.

One of the reasons women don't ask, she argues, is that they don't realize that opportunities exist. Babcock writes, "One of the major barriers preventing women from asking for what they need more of the time is their perception that their circumstances are more fixed and absolute—less negotiable—than they really are."

I just felt lucky to have the opportunity.
—SHERYL SANDBERG

Now a household name, Sheryl Sandberg has achieved extraordinary success in her career to date. When she agreed to talk to me for this book, I actually got nervous. Surely her experiences must be very different. What if she debunked all my theories?

Sandberg served as chief of staff for the United States Department of the Treasury before leaving government to become vice president of global online sales and operations at Google. She's now the chief operating officer of the social networking giant Facebook and the founder of Leanin.org. Sandberg clearly knows her stuff about gender dynamics as well as social media.

When I ask whether she believes my struggle to be fairly compensated is a common problem, she immediately agrees: "The data clearly show men own their success more than women do. Men are more likely to overestimate and women are more likely to underestimate performance on objective criteria. So if you look at something like grade point average and you survey men and women on what their GPAs were, men get it wrong slightly high and women get it wrong slightly low."

So men are more likely to think of themselves as more successful and women are more likely to think of themselves as less successful, even if their achievements are the same. Sandberg also points out that men ascribe their success to their own skills, whereas women ascribe their success to outside sources.

"So if you ask a man, 'Why were you successful?' the man will say, 'You know, because of myself,'" Sandberg says. "And the women will say, 'Because I got lucky and these great people I work with helped me.' So think of the situation in which men are getting it wrong slightly high, and women slightly low. Men think it's them; women don't. So why does that matter? It matters because I think a lot of getting ahead in the workplace has to do with being willing to raise your hand and say I want that job, I'll take on that challenge—or better yet, I see that problem and I'm going to fix it. That comes back to self-confidence. So when men feel more confident they raise their hand; when women feel less confident they take their hand down."

A lot of getting ahead in the workplace has to do
with being willing to raise your hand.
—SHERYL SANDBERG

Knowing your value means owning your success. Owning your success means acknowledging your achievements. By acknowledging achievements you build confidence.

Sandberg gives me a striking example from her own experience. She was giving a talk about owning one's success to 150 or so Facebook employees, and she mentioned the GPA experiment. At the end of the talk, Sandberg told the audience she had time for two more questions. She answered them, but hands were waving, so she continued to call on people.

Afterward she went back to her desk and found a young woman waiting for her. Sandberg asked if she'd learned anything from the talk, and the young woman said, "I learned to keep my hand up." Sandberg asked what she meant, and the woman told her, "After you took those two final questions, I put my hand down and all the other women put their hands down. A bunch of men kept their hands up and then you took more questions."

The men ignored the question limit and went for it, keeping their hands in the air. What did they have to lose? Nothing. Sandberg saw more waving hands and took their questions.

Sandberg admits she didn't notice that only women had taken their hands down, because after all, why would she have noticed what wasn't there? She says that proved her point right there: "If we as women don't raise our hands in the workplace, we're not going to get the same opportunities men do. Because men keep their hands up."

Despite her many achievements, Sandberg tells me a story of how she herself failed to raise her hand and how it almost cost her a lot of money.

"I was getting a new position. I got an offer to do the job, and I thought the offer was really great, and I was going to take it," Sandberg says. "My brother-in-law kept saying, 'You gotta negotiate. They want you to take on all this responsibility—ask for more compensation.' My response was, 'This is such a great opportunity. I'm so lucky to get it, and it's such a generous offer, I'm not going to negotiate.'" But Sandberg says her brother-in-law kept pushing: "He said, 'Goddamn it, Sheryl, why are you agreeing to make half of what any man would make to do this?'"

Finally, that motivated her. Sandberg says that after her brother-in-law convinced her to ask for more, "I went in and asked, and they moved up considerably. Had I not asked, they wouldn't have. But the reason I wouldn't have asked is because I just felt lucky to have the opportunity." Her story sounded all too familiar to me. I've always been in awe of Sandberg, and the idea that she and I shared a common failing was cracking the superhero image I had of her. I appreciate her honesty. And I realize now that women must get over feeling lucky. The time has come to turn the page.

Sandberg sent my daughters and me some Facebook T-shirts. I wear mine feeling a kinship with this powerful woman, who didn't know her "face" value, even as she reached the top of the ladder.

I was just happy to have the professional position.
—CAROL BARTZ

Carol Bartz, who was the president and CEO of Yahoo! when I interviewed her for the original *Know Your Value*, was also an eye-opener. To borrow the famous line from the movie *When Harry Met Sally*, "I'll have what she's having!"

Bartz was a rarity in today's corporate world: during her time as CEO, she was among the select women heading 3 percent of Fortune

500 companies and one of only a handful heading a technology firm. When I ask her whether she has ever had trouble getting paid what she's worth, her reply is immediate: "Oh, honest to god, I think every step of the way. There's no question about that."

Bartz tells me that in the early 1990s, she was competing with two men to be CEO of Autodesk, a multinational design software company. She got the job and ended up with what she thought was a generous compensation package. But she later found out that the men she was up against had been asking for millions more. Says Bartz: "What they were negotiating for was way over—way over what they had negotiated with me . . . you know, I was too naïve, too stupid, and they got me on the cheap . . . when I found out what the guys were asking, I thought, 'You dummy.'"

Bartz says that early on in her career, she had difficulty promoting herself. "When I was younger, I was just happy to have the professional position," she tells me. "Then I think you naïvely put your head in the sand, and think they will notice your worth."

I was struck by the fact that both Bartz and Sandberg were telling me stories about not knowing their value, and feeling lucky to get the offers they did. I had assumed their psychology would be different, and that they had handled themselves very differently. Hearing these women talk about luck struck a chord with me. My feeling lucky to have a job had cost me dearly over the years. Feeling lucky and fearing rejection. Women who run women's magazines are extremely in tune with those sentiments that drive us or get in our way. On this issue, they let it rip.

Lesley Jane Seymour, former editor-in-chief of More magazine, is now the founder of CoveyClub, a forthcoming online networking site for women who are forty or more and thriving.

She is a wife and mom, and she is also a friend and mentor.

She tells me, "If you talk to a lot of women as you're doing this, you're going to hear a lot of women use the word luck. I hear executives all the time say, 'I'm lucky to have gotten here, I'm lucky' . . . I can't even tell you how many successful females, CEOs of companies, will say 'I just got lucky.' But if you think it's just luck that made you successful, then if you ask for too much, the luck might just run out."

"Emotion can trip women up," Seymour says when she hears my story. "We are willing to take those substitutes because we have been brought up on emotion." Seymour, who has run several magazines in the thirty-some years she's been in publishing, said it took her years to realize that feeling "loved" by her bosses did not mean she was being valued. "I definitely made the mistake in my career of looking for an emotional connection instead of just money. I used to tell my boss that I would do the job 'even if you didn't pay me,'" Seymour says, laughing. "I guess they decided to take me at my word." She would later discover that colleagues with the same responsibilities had larger salaries.

We are willing to take those substitutes
because we have been brought up on emotion.
—LESLEY JANE SEYMOUR

"I ran each magazine basically with the idea I was going to run it as if it were my own product, my own business, with my own money . . . I'm going to make the best choices because I'm running it as if it's mine, I'm putting in 120 hours a week, and I'm saving them money, they're going to love me so much . . . and guess what. They didn't care!"

Seymour says her bosses quickly figured out that she'd accept approval instead of money. "I had one boss who was very good. For instance, once when I had a really good year, she took me out to lunch and she gave me a pair of earrings. Jeweled earrings. She told me how much the company loved me. That was very smart. That's something that women are susceptible to. No man is going to take another man out to lunch, give him a pair of earrings, and say how much the company loves him. The guy would say 'What's wrong with this company?' I mean, my husband would laugh hysterically and walk out. His response would be, 'What kind of company is this? Give me a raise!' Instead, my first reaction was, 'Oh my god, thank you, you love me so much!'"

Bottom line, says Seymour: "The men's way of doing business is without emotion. It's just money. It's just business. Emotions play absolutely no hand in business in America in general. You have to bring as little emotion as you can to it."

Senior Vice President and Chief Human Resources Officer at Independence Blue Cross, Jeanie Heffernan, sees how emotions impact women at work on a daily basis, often in a negative way. But unlike Seymour, she suggests that emotions do have a place, if you focus on the right ones. When defining the line, she says, "I think it's okay to show emotion if you are showing empathy, compassion. If you're able to relate to somebody's situation—like a loss, for instance—then it's okay to let that emotion translate to the individual so they can see and hear that you are legitimately and authentically feeling for them. So I do think emotion is okay. We are people, we have emotions, we are not robots. If we all walk around robotically, then we are losing something."

And one of the best emotions to bring to the workplace? Passion.

"The passion piece is huge. I think that is a positive—when you can actually see someone's passion regarding a topic or the mission of the organization. That could be really good, but like anything else, there should be balance to the passion; you can't be over the top [without seeming myopic]. It is all about moderation."

> *You can't expect men to take us seriously*
> *if we don't take ourselves seriously. That is just the truth.*
> *It would be sweet if they did.* —NORA EPHRON

My friend, the extremely talented late Nora Ephron (1941–2012), was a movie director, producer, screenwriter, author, and playwright. I am beyond thankful that I had the chance to interview her for the first edition of this book before she passed away. She told me, "I think several things are truer about women than they are about men in terms of knowing your value. One is that women have a constitutional resistance to quitting. We like to be good. We like to be loyal. We like to be good girls. One of the ways you make more money in the workplace is by quitting and going someplace else. It's always been my feeling that women just don't get that; they don't learn that lesson that men constantly teach, which is you have to keep moving in order to get raises."

Ephron said this was true of her early career, when she was working at *Esquire* magazine. She was thrilled to be working there, even though she was being paid something like $1,000 per month. "I was married at the time, and I didn't have to make a lot of money because there were two incomes," she says. "Then my marriage broke up, and the editor of *New York* magazine called and offered me three times as much as I was making at *Esquire*. First of all I needed the money, but second of all I was so stunned by it. I went to the editor of *Esquire* and I said, 'I've had this offer from *New York* magazine.' And he said, 'We'll match it.' Then I got really irritated, because I thought, 'Why did I have to ask for this?' And then after I got done thinking that, I thought, 'Well it's my fault—I should have asked for it!'"

In hindsight, Ephron told me she just wasn't taking herself as seriously as she should have. She didn't know her value, and to some degree she didn't care, because she was so happy to be working at that particular magazine. Ultimately she went to *New York* magazine simply because she was so annoyed that she'd been underpaid and had worked for so long without realizing it.

Ephron did not blame women, but explained to me the problem is that "we don't take ourselves seriously. We can't expect men to take us seriously if we don't take ourselves seriously. That is just the truth. It would be sweet if they did and we didn't have to do anything. But that's what we want; we don't want to have to do anything. We don't want people thinking that we're pushy or masculine."

Arianna Huffington—high-profile columnist, author, and co-founder and editor-in-chief of *The Huffington Post*—has been a friend and a supporter of mine since *Morning Joe* began. She agrees that asking for a raise is an area fraught with anxiety for many women. "One reason is that most women have a very different relationship to money than men do," she tells me. "For us, money represents love, power, security, control, self-worth, independence. After all, if money were just money, everyone would always make rational decisions about it. And we know women certainly don't always do that. But why? One reason is that women have been raised to think of money in terms of security—and not just financial security. Even today, a surprising number of us still think that it's the man's job to make and understand money. Far too often we delegate this responsibility and don't learn enough about money—so of course we fear it."

Women don't say what they think, and
they don't do what they feel. —SUZE ORMAN

After she hears my story, financial guru, talk-show host, author, and motivational speaker Suze Orman puts it succinctly: "The problem is, a woman is socialized to accept that which she is given. So if somebody tells you that you can't, you believe it. If somebody says you're not worth it, you believe it. You get angry, but you can't say anything because women don't say what they think and they don't do what they feel."

Wanting to be liked, taking things personally, feeling lucky to have the job, fearing unknown consequences: these are filters through which a lot of women view their work, and that influences the way they react. But the truth is, the filters blur our focus and keep us from our goals.

Looking back at the Paris Hilton incident and the events that followed, I realize it is just one of many cautionary tales I have to share. I would like my story to speak to any and all younger or newly employed women who feel they are "just lucky to be there." Get over being so grateful for the opportunity. If you're good, you should know it and own it, and always be ready to walk. Always be aware of your ability to walk. Depend on no one to notice your worth. Being liked should not be your first priority. I am one hundred percent sure, looking back now, that had I reacted differently when I received my admonition/promotion, my fate would have been different, too. That manager probably would have had more respect for me if I hadn't apologized for ripping up the script. I should have said that I respectfully disagreed with her assessment of the incident, and I should have seized the opportunity to ask for more money. Instead, I did what was asked of me.

CHAPTER 3

WHAT'S A WOMAN WORTH?

The Gender Wage Gap and the Perception of Value

My story, with Marie C. Wilson, Ilene H. Lang, Brian Nosek, Tina Brown,

Jack Welch, Donny Deutsch, Susie Essman, Senator Claire McCaskill,

Brooksley Born, Sheila Bair, and Hannah Riley Bowles

Not Yet Equal

One could easily argue that women have made impressive gains over the past fifty years. Yes, women now make up more than half the workforce. Yes, we are governors of states and have run for president. Yes, there are three women on the Supreme Court, and women are commanding space shuttles and serving on Navy submarines. Women in the United States are better educated than men: they receive three college degrees for every two that men earn, they earn more master's degrees than men do, and about 43 percent of all MBAs. But despite all these impressive gains, we still sell ourselves way too short. According to the United States Labor Department data, women earned approximately 83 cents for every dollar their male counterparts made in 2016.

Women are not just lagging in wages; they are far behind when it comes to leadership. Women make up only 19 percent of the United States Congress. The United States ranks 104th of 190 countries in terms of the proportion of women in their national legislatures—behind France and even Afghanistan and Pakistan. Across such industries as business, law, academia, journalism, and politics, on average, women hold fewer than 20 percent of the top positions. Only 6.4 percent of *Fortune* 500 companies have female CEOs. This number has gone up from 3 percent in the time since the first edition of this book was written, but the numbers are still frustratingly low. So if women are now 50 percent of the workforce, why aren't more women in charge?

Problem? What Problem?

The truth is that the general populace thinks women are already leading across all sectors of the economy. "That's what Deborah Rhode, a scholar at Stanford, wrote of this phenomenon [more than] a decade ago, and it's still true," says women's advocate Marie C. Wilson.

Wilson is a co-creator of Take Our Daughters and Sons to Work Day® and founder and president of the White House Project, a national nonpartisan nonprofit that aims to advance women's leadership in all communities and sectors. The problem, she explained, is that if people think women have already reached parity, the political will doesn't exist to continue fighting for change. "Even though the majority of Americans are comfortable with women leading in all sectors, women's leadership numbers are static at an average of 18 percent across all ten examined sectors," Wilson says. "When we have actually gotten small groups of CEOs together and interviewed them about why there are not more women leading, they will say, 'I'm not comfortable—I'm just not comfortable.' Some of that is because there are so few women, they think they're going to say the wrong thing."

She suggests that men may be hesitant to give women direct feedback for fear of retaliatory lawsuits. And there just aren't enough women leading to fundamentally change the dynamic.

Wilson says that "the magic number seems to be 33 percent. If you have one-third women, like you now have on the Supreme Court, it starts to not be about gender, it starts to be about what each of us is talking about. Until you have one-third, you are still looked at through a gender lens."

None of this comes as a surprise to women themselves. As columnist Lisa Belkin noted in a *New York Times Magazine* article, "Telling women they have reached parity is like telling an unemployed worker the recession is over. It isn't true until it feels true." Most women can tell you from personal experience that they've been paid less than men for the same work.

Researchers agree that a lot of the gender wage gap is explainable. Women take time off to have children, so their careers are interrupted and they're not putting in the same number of hours. Women are the caregivers—they're more likely to be the ones taking care of the kids, their aging parents, and their extended family. They also do the majority of housework even when they're the primary breadwinners. Men will choose higher-paying occupations and women will choose more portable (and lower-paying) occupations that allow them to move with a higher-earning spouse. So conventional wisdom says women don't commit as strongly to the labor market, and as a result, they don't earn as much over the course of a lifetime.

But women's choices don't explain everything. "What you find is that when you pull out all of those factors, you still have about 40 percent of the wage gap—9.2 cents—unexplained," says Ariane Hegewisch, a study director at the Institute for Women's Policy Research.

Subconscious Bias

The sad fact is that both men and women are more likely to consider men to be valuable employees. Researchers referred to one experiment in particular that's been repeated in many different places. Ilene H. Lang, a former tech CEO and chief executive officer of Catalyst, a leading research organization that studies women in the workforce, summed up the findings this way: "Basically, if you take resumes and strip them of names and all gender information, then take the exact same resumes and put a man's name on some with links to a man, and put a woman's name on others with links to a woman, and send them out, hiring managers say that the women are unqualified and the men are terrific candidates. Men get the promotion or job and the women do not. Once you attach a gender link or a gender label, it gets devalued if it's female. This happens over and over again, and it is not because people are intentionally biased or intentionally sexist, but they do not see potential and leadership in women, particularly nonwhite women."

What was really shocking to me was the fact that women were as likely as men to ascribe leadership qualities to men, and dismiss equally qualified women.

Brian Nosek is the director of Project Implicit, a collaboration of scientists at Harvard, the University of Washington, and the University of Virginia. The project uses an online word association test to gauge subconscious bias. For instance, the test measures how quickly you pair words such as male and career. (The test is online, and anyone can take it: https:implicit.harvard.edu.) When I took it I found that—even though I was writing this book—I, too, subconsciously associate males with career and females with family.

Nosek says these subconscious beliefs could manifest themselves in a variety of ways. For example, "[a manager] may be less likely to ask a female staff member to take a job that requires travel, whereas the same thought might not occur to a manager with a male staffer." And, Nosek points out, this can happen whether the manager is a man or a woman.

When I ask how this might have an impact on my quest for a raise, Nosek says, "The way in which this implicit stereotype might manifest is just a general feeling of not belonging, an uncertainty that this is something I am, or can do . . . whether it's appropriate to even ask, whereas it may not occur to a man in the same situation to even think about whether it's appropriate or not. He might think, 'I've been working here three years—time for a raise, damn it!'"

I ask former Catalyst President and CEO Ilene H. Lang why women just aren't seen as leaders. One of the reasons, she says, is that bias is perpetuated by the workplace itself. Her organization studied how employees are chosen in companies that have leadership-development programs. "Most companies have competency-based models . . . they start out by saying, 'Who's successful in our company? What do those successful leaders in our company look like?'" Lang tells me. The companies then design their program for screening high-potential individuals around those key attributes. But because subconscious bias plays its part, the companies end up institutionalizing a preference for men.

"The performance-management system will say, 'This is how we spot the up-and-coming talent; these are the things you have to be good at,' and, well, when you look at most of those characteristics, what you find is that of the top ten, six or seven reflect characteristics of the current leadership, which is most often male," she says.

Like many of us, Tina Brown sees the institutionalized preference for men in action all the time. "You discover with a sort of incredulity that men don't even picture a woman in a job." She offers a recent example in which she was talking to a television executive about staffing changes at his organization: "I asked, 'Who are you thinking of bringing in to be the overall boss of the situation?' And he looked around the room, and he said, 'Well, I was thinking about maybe somebody like—' and he named a guy who was a complete mid-level player, in my judgment. I was incredulous. I'm thinking, 'Wait a minute. Within this organization that we're discussing, I could think of three brilliant women who could easily do that job. They're not even on the drawing board. He's thinking about going outside to a mid-level man who's had a lot of corporate buzz and he's ignoring the three women in the company who I know for a fact are far superior.'"

Behind the Starting Line

What surprised me most was the news that most women, even if they get their well-deserved raise, won't ever close the wage gap. Even if women get promotions and raises at the same rate as men, if in their first job they were placed at a lower position and salary than their male colleagues, the same promotion and compensation increase rates will not close the gap. Ilene H. Lang points to a Catalyst study of female and male MBA graduates. "Women are pegged at a lower level and lower salary from the very first job out of their MBA program if they start at entry level. If they are hired at a mid-career level, women and men fare pretty much the same, and they track the same afterward. But somehow, at that entry level, men are seen as much more promising and much more valuable, just because they're men. More women take a hit, just because they're women." So that's hidden bias in action, and where the gender wage gap begins to grow. Says Lang: "The metaphor I use is, imagine that there's a big race and your daughter or your granddaughter or your sister—whoever it is—is really good at track and field and she's training, and she trains with the best of them. She goes to the start line, and you look up and she's not on the start line. She's 100 feet back. Would you accept this? So that's the challenge: women are starting out behind the start line. And they don't catch up."

Women are starting out behind the start line.
And they don't catch up. —ILENE H. LANG

But Aren't Women Good for Business?

These gender disparities exist despite studies that suggest having more women in the top spots boosts the bottom line. That's why the European telecommunications giant Deutsche Telekom mandates that one-third of its top jobs be filled by women. The company's CEO said in a statement, "Taking on more women in management positions is not about the enforcement of misconstrued egalitarianism; having more women at the top will simply help us operate better."

A study by the University of British Columbia's Sauder School of Business found that female CEOs and female company directors tend to pay less in corporate takeovers, creating less debt and saving their shareholders money. Research shows that when more women are on the board of directors, companies are less likely to pay those outrageous compensations we've heard so much about on the news. That's why Norway put a law on the books requiring that at least 40 percent of the boards of directors of public companies be female.

Much of the research about gender and performance, however, is still under debate. Academics who challenge the current findings ask, "If companies that hire more women do better, how do we really know what role women play in that success? Are companies that seek out divergent perspectives simply more innovative and therefore make more money?"

Curiously, two men I interviewed—both of them tremendously successful captains of industry—argued that there's no substantial difference between male and female executives at the very top. But Jack Welch argues that the best corporate leaders are gender-neutral.

> *When you get a good woman leader,*
> *she is every bit as good as a man . . .*
> *good leaders are gender-neutral.*
> **—JACK WELCH**

In his twenty years as CEO of General Electric, the parent company of NBC, Jack Welch was credited with turning that company into one of America's largest and most valuable. His management skills are legendary and earned him a reputation as one of America's toughest bosses. If his managers weren't producing, they no longer had a job.

I present Welch with the theory I'd heard from other interviewees—that executives love hiring women because women work harder and aren't always asking for things like bigger offices and more money, and they don't spend a lot of time drawing attention to themselves and self-promoting. Does he agree?

Welch takes the contrarian point of view: "I think the distinction in many ways is a phony distinction. A players, really great managers and leaders, are almost gender-neutral. When you get a good woman leader, she is every bit as good as a man and has many of the same characteristics. One thing I would say is that certain industries are much more amenable to women leaders and they all will be eventually . . . but good leaders are gender-neutral."

Welch believes that truly great executives don't even have to take their gender into consideration. "They're comfortable with their gender, male or female. They're not going to mask one or the other," he says.

Or could it be that truly great female executives navigate gender differences so instinctively and effectively that the men don't notice? I have to believe that women bring different abilities and sensibilities to their work, and in many cases that works to their advantage, and to their company's advantage. Gender research is ongoing, but anecdotal evidence is a powerful thing. All the other women—and men—I spoke with pointed to the fact that women are simply more collaborative.

Give me a man and a woman of the same talent,
and I will take the woman every single time.
—DONNY DEUTSCH

"Surrounding myself with women is a real key to my success," Donny Deutsch tells me. Of course he said that! If you've seen Deutsch on *Morning Joe*, you know that we have an ongoing on-air joke about his attitude toward women. He even bought me a pair of $800 shoes to "buy back" my favor after insulting me on air with sarcastic remarks that some regarded as borderline misogynistic. I have since given the shoes away. They are ridiculously high . . . and they don't match my message.

But Deutsch does have valuable contributions to make to this conversation. The chairman of a multibillion-dollar advertising agency, he has big money to match his big personality and fancy wardrobe. The man thinks big, and he explains how I can too.

"Give me a man and a woman of the same talent, and I will take the woman every single time," he says.

Why? He tells me to take a look at advertising: "If you watch little girls in a Saturday morning TV commercial for a Barbie, game, or anything, it's always the same: it's three or four girls sitting around a kitchen table playing together collaboratively—that's the commercial. If you watch a commercial for a little boys' game or toy, at the end one boy always raises his fists: 'I won!' I think in many ways senior women executives are superior in that, for them, it's not a zero-sum game. They want to work collaboratively, they want to support, they want to be part of the team. It's not as much about how big is my paycheck, how big is my office. . . ."

His is a mixed message: on one hand, Deutsch says, yes, women may want to be liked, and yes, they do the invisible jobs; that's why he likes women, that's why they are valuable employees. But it is the next words out of his mouth that explain why women so often end up with much of the work and little of the glory: "What I have also found is that—once again, this is not a rule either, there are exceptions to it—but for that very reason sometimes men have made better CEOs because that charge-the-hill aggression, that 'what's in it for me,' the very thing that makes it harder to manage them is what makes them better in the top spot."

I tell Deutsch that there are feminists who are not going to like what he says.

"I'm the ultimate feminist," he fires back. "Eight out of my ten senior partners are women. This is a company I built; the CEO is a woman, the CFO is a woman . . . I'm just saying that some of the time the things that make women more successful in the most senior positions can also work against them."

Although I don't like hearing it, I appreciate Deutsch's honesty. And he's certainly right: women need to get better at charging the hill. I hear essentially the same message from everyone I speak with. Deutsch is simply being generous enough to tell the truth: either we own our value and get to the top, or we can work hard and let the men take the credit.

Most everyone also agreed that women just work harder. Certainly I was working as hard as my cohost, and harder than all the other men around me, though I was getting nowhere.

"It's the Fred Astaire–Ginger Rogers thing," Ilene H. Lang says after I recount my story. "Women do the same steps as men, but they do them backwards and in high heels. That's what women have to go through to show that they're as good as men. They have to work harder, they take much longer to be promoted, and they have to prove themselves over and over again."

I always felt like I had to be so much better, and
in a way that did me a favor. —SUSIE ESSMAN

My friend and frequent *Morning Joe* guest Susie Essman may be better known as Susie Green, the foul-mouthed ball-breaking character she plays on the critically acclaimed HBO series *Curb Your Enthusiasm*. But Essman isn't anything like her alter ego Green, who tells her husband to go F himself if she doesn't get what she wants; the real Essman says that despite her success, she is nagged by the feeling that she has to keep proving herself.

Essman has spent most of her career as a stand-up comic. "Talk about a boys' club!" she says of the 1980s New York City comedy circuit. Essman says because the clubs hired mostly men, women had a hard time getting on stage at all, let alone at a decent hour. Women, she says, were often relegated to performing in the wee hours of the morning.

"I always felt like I had to be so much better, and in a way that did me a favor," Essman tells me. "Instead of saying, 'Oh, they're not going to give me a good spot in the clubs because I'm a female,' I was going to be so good they couldn't deny me.

"Was it fair? No. But life isn't fair," Essman says. "I remember that my dad, who was a physician, told me, 'Whenever you go to the doctor, go to a female doctor because they have to work so much harder to get where they are that they're probably better.'"

One of my favorite senators, Claire McCaskill (D-MO), has spent decades proving herself in the male-dominated world of American politics. When I ask which areas of the economy could benefit from a greater number of women, she tells me, "It is my observation that the women who have done well have been hyperprepared. Being prepared means completely understanding what you're doing. I've always had the feeling someone is going to tap me on the shoulder and say, 'What are you doing here?' So I wanted to be prepared when they did; I wanted to know the answer. And if there's anything that the Wall Street meltdown showed us, it's that a lot of people were engaging in complex financial interactions that they didn't completely understand. My observation is, perhaps if there were more women on board saying, 'Wait a minute, are we sure we understand what this actually is?', then maybe it might have slowed down the train."

There's also the feeling that women, especially when they're in the minority, offer fresh perspective. As I interviewed highly successful women in finance and government, I began to wonder if being in the minority might sometimes work to their advantage.

That's often the case on *Morning Joe*. On days when I'm outnumbered by men, when, for example, Donny Deutsch, Steve Rattner, Mark Halperin, and of course Willie and Joe, get on a testosterone-fueled roll, I'm the one to say, "Hold the phone."

(These days, there are fewer testosterone-fests on the show: we have more women at the table than ever and they KILL it. Katty Kay, Nicole Wallace, Heidi Przybyla, Yamiche Alcindor, Elise Jordan, Susan Del Percio, and Kasie Hunt . . . just to name a few.)

The absence of women in the top spots on Wall Street was blatantly obvious at the height of the financial crisis. If you turned on the television news in the middle of it all, you'll probably recall that iconic scene of the seven heads of the biggest banks hauled before Congress. One couldn't help but notice the total lack of diversity in that line-up.

Some behavioral economists believe there are biological reasons men make crazy bets. Joe Herbert, a neuroscientist at Cambridge University who studied the effects of testosterone on stock traders, told *New York* magazine, "The banking crisis was caused by doing what no society ever allows: permitting young males to behave in an unregulated way. Anyone who studied neurobiology would have predicted disaster."

Headlines such as *New York* magazine's "What If Women Ran Wall Street?" and the *Washington Post*'s "In Banking Crisis, Guys Get the Blame, More Women Needed in Top Jobs, Critics Say" promoted the idea that we all might benefit from having more women in positions of power on Wall Street.

Would Wall Street have crumbled in 2008 if women were running the show? I ask both Brooksley Born, former chair of the Commodity Futures Trading Commission, and Sheila Bair, 19th chair of the Federal Deposit Insurance Corporation. Both are rarities in the world of government: They've held powerful positions overseeing the banking industry, they famously clashed with Wall Street during their tenure as financial regulators, and both are well-known for displaying political bravery in their (ultimately unsuccessful) attempts to warn the country of looming threats to the American economy. As head of the CFTC during the Clinton administration, Born was among the first to call for greater disclosure and regulation of the rapidly growing market in financial derivatives. As head of the FDIC, the government agency that regulates banks and insures depositors, Sheila Bair was a prominent figure in the economic meltdown and was also recognized for her early attempt to get the second Bush administration to address the imminent subprime mortgage crisis.

Neither is willing to categorize women as less likely to be risk takers. Both point to the fact that women in the finance world are outsiders, however, and to some degree that fact helped them bring a new perspective to bear on the industry's problems.

Born says, "You know, I've read these studies about risk taking, but I don't have the expertise to evaluate them. I do think that if you are a bit of an outsider, which certainly a woman in that position [as a government banking regulator] was then, and to some extent is now, you may not be blinded by the conventional wisdom, or the group-think, that is the views held by your peers. You obviously aren't part of the club and therefore don't have pressure to remain in everybody's good graces in quite the same way. Maybe you can analyze things a little independently, and if you come to a different conclusion than the others, maybe you have the courage to express that conclusion."

But the flip side of that coin is, if you are an outsider, nobody's taking you seriously. Born was trained as a lawyer, not a banker, and she acknowledges that that played a role in her inability to force change: "I was not from Wall Street, which many of them were. And in fact, many of them were from the very highest ranks of Wall Street. And that, in and of itself, was a bit of a club, to which I did not belong. . . . I also think that they all knew each other to some extent from their previous lives. They didn't know me. I was in a small agency, much smaller than any of the other financial regulatory agencies. It had traditionally been a rather weak agency, a backwater if you will, that happened to oversee derivatives. And in fact, I think [the fact that the agency was a backwater] may have been the reason why, in that era, some women had been head of the CFTC, but no women had been chair of the SEC or of the Fed."

Sheila Bair echoes Born's sentiments. "I do think that to the extent you let outsiders into the financial sector, that's good, and it really is a club world . . . to the extent women have been outsiders, getting them in to take fresh looks and offer fresh perspectives is very helpful." Did being the rare female working in finance put her at a disadvantage when she was calling for reform in the subprime mortgage market? "The media and others have focused on my gender," she explains, "but I think just as relevant is that I am a Midwesterner, and I graduated from a public university, so I was never part of the East Coast, New York financial establishment. I think my frankness was unusual, as was my outspokenness, particularly coming from the FDIC, which has historically taken a back seat among financial regulators. While some may have focused on my gender, I think my views may have been too much, too soon, for others to adopt them."

I argue that as outsiders in the world of high finance, women like Born and Bair can think more clearly and offer new insights. But in practice, if you're an outsider and nobody's taking your perspective seriously, your insights have no effect because nobody hears you. When I give her my reasoning, Born says, "Exactly. That's the problem!"

Professor Hannah Riley Bowles studies gender in negotiation and leadership at Harvard University. She describes diversity as a double-edged sword: "Diverse teams often perform better than teams that are less diverse," but only if people in the workplace actually value diversity and want to benefit from the fact that dissimilar people will bring alternate experiences and viewpoints to bear on their input. "If you're in a context where people say things like 'diversity doesn't matter, we're really all the same around here, we're color blind, gender blind,' or whatever, then people feel self-conscious about their differences. Then those differences become suppressed, and the potential for communication failures increases," she says, citing research done by Robin Ely and David Thomas at Harvard Business School. Born's and Bair's unheeded warnings about potentially cataclysmic banking practices could be considered communication failures of the greatest degree.

> *There is nothing more important than*
> *waking up in the morning and saying,*
> *"I count. I matter—what I can contribute,*
> *what I can provide, what I can accomplish."*
> —VICTORIA BUDSON

I recently spoke with founding executive director of the Women and Public Policy Program at Harvard University (WAPPP) Victoria Budson and asked for her thoughts on how women impact their organization's bottom line. WAPPP is the preeminent institution for forwarding research on ways of closing gender gaps, educating students and leaders on gender policy, and implementing policy changes at local, state, and national levels.

Budson underscored the undeniable economic impact of gender diversity: "We could talk about it from the frame of equity, or the ethics of ensuring that everyone has an equal opportunity. . . . But initially, [recognizing the contributions of women] is important, because if we are going to have the major advances in the artificial intelligence revolution, in all of the tech, hardware, software that are developed . . . if we don't have women within those organizations, the chance of having the same level of innovation gets diminished. Because we are missing 51 percent of both the talent pool, but also the market. So companies that have people who represent broad cross-sections of the marketplace, who are designing products and taking things to market, definitely do better."

Budson also left me with an important mantra: "Men value themselves, so women should value themselves even in the face of societal cues that tell women not to. In every culture and every society in the world, women are signaled to not value themselves. There is nothing more important than waking up in the morning and saying, 'I count. I matter—what I can contribute, what I can provide, what I can accomplish.'"

Obviously there are still major obstacles that keep women from achieving parity in the workplace. But were my own problems caused by gender bias? Have I been discriminated against in my career? Probably, somewhere along the line. But being angry and blaming men (and even high-level women) for holding me back isn't constructive. I take full responsibility, and therefore full credit, for my career. My feeling is, I can only control what I can control. Instead of just being frustrated about the wage disparities that exist in my field, I'd rather think about what I can do within the parameters of my situation. When it came time to take drastic action to resolve my salary problem, I wanted to find ways to take matters into my own hands.

CHAPTER 4

ACCEPTABLE BEHAVIOR

A Cautionary Tale About Women Acting Like Men in the Workplace

My story, with Donny Deutsch, Hannah Riley Bowles, Jack Welch, Carol Bartz, Joy Behar, Sheryl Sandberg, Sheila Bair, Susie Essman, Marie C. Wilson, and Arianna Huffington

Acting Like a Man

For months I had watched Joe cut his own deals and get what he needed for the show. Getting what he wanted meant engaging in loud battles with Phil Griffin on a regular basis. Phil was extremely close to Joe; they had worked together for years.

Often I'd be sitting between them as it began. They'd lean past me and get in each other's face. Invariably the exchange started like this: Joe wants to hire a certain producer or writer or analyst. Phil says no, there is no money. The volume goes up. Then they stand. Then fingers start pointing. There's shouting. Growling. Even threatening. Joe threatening to quit; Phil threatening to fire him. Neither of them meaning it. I watch spit splatter on the coffee table in front of me—I can actually hear it hit the table. *Splat!* As I study the drops, more come raining down.

Soon they get up and stand face-to-face, me sitting awkwardly between them on the couch. They lean in over me, poking each other in the chest, with their faces red and inches apart. Then, as my own stress level escalates to its highest point, there's a miraculous pivot.

One of Joe's talents: diffusing a moment within a blink of an eye.

Joe offers to hug Phil and then fires one last question at him.

"Phil, how the hell can the Mets win the World Series when their pitching is so spotty?"

Phil responds as if the two had been calmly talking sports the whole time. As the spit dries on the table, they sit down and continue with a calm and friendly conversation.

That would never happen with a woman. Never in a million years. No woman could survive a scene like that with her boss. Yet whenever Phil and Joe are negotiating, the drill is the same: they yell, spit, scream, and slam phones down. They each walk away with what they want, and their relationship remains intact. In fact, it's better. They'll have something to laugh about later over a beer.

I remember once when Phil was screaming, and Joe hung up on him. Phil didn't realize that Joe had hung up, so he continued to scream until his assistant knocked on the door and told him that Joe had hung up four minutes ago. Phil was so amused by that that he called Joe back to laugh about it: "F—cker, you wouldn't believe what just happened, I was screaming and you hung up and I didn't know that for four minutes! That's hysterical . . . so what were we talking about? Oh right, yeah sure. I'll give you the extra producer."

After months of watching how Joe's aggressive, in-your-face method seemed to get him what he needed, I decided I'd give it a try.

I went into Phil's office and sat down on his couch and proceeded to tell him in no uncertain terms that my salary was a joke and that he'd better change it.

"I'm really, really tired of not being paid my worth," I said angrily. "You keep saying you will deal with it. When Phil, when? This is ridiculous, and I am not going to put up with it anymore." I raised my voice and tossed in a few F-bombs.

The approach was very Joe. Except I am not Joe, and this was not me: my eyes were open a bit too wide; my heart was beating fast, my body shook. My voice rose into the upper register. Higher pitched. Pushing it.

Somehow we ended up standing next to his door, and I was six inches from his face saying something like, "How could you let me be in this position? Seriously Phil, seriously! You need to fix this!"

I wish I could erase this entire scene from my memory, and his. The whole thing was a bad idea. Needless to say, I didn't walk out with a raise. While Joe and many other men could pull this off, I wasn't believable in any way.

We "bro," it gets out, and that's it. —DONNY DEUTSCH

A *New York* magazine profile on Donny Deutsch and life at his ad agency described an argument between Deutsch and one of his male employees: "We were screaming. Our noses were touching. Then we started laughing."

I ask Deutsch about that episode, and he explains to me, "We 'bro,' it gets out, and that's it."

So why, I ask incredulously, didn't that work for me?

"Because it was a side Phil wasn't used to seeing. He was threatened, and he didn't know how to handle it," Deutsch answers. "If a woman punches you, you don't know what to do. You can't hit a woman back. If she punches you, you think, 'What's wrong with her?'"

Harvard professor Hannah Riley Bowles says another reason my tack did not work is simply that I didn't have the same relationship with Phil that Joe has. "It's generally the case that people tend to know better and hang around with and be closer to people who are like them. Right?" she reasons. "So the implication of that in a male-dominated industry is that guys will tend to be very well-connected with guys. Their social network and their work network will tend to be overwhelmingly male."

Research done by Herminia Ibarra at the INSEAD business school found that men are more likely to be connected to more senior male executives by virtue of the fact that they're both male. By contrast, women tend to have both male and female colleagues in their work networks, but their networks of close friends are likely to be mostly women and friends from outside of work. "So if you have someone who is a friend and a colleague, you can speak to them and relate to them in ways that you cannot with someone with whom you have a more distant, or just really collegial, relationship," Bowles tells me. She says the difference is that in a male-dominated industry, men typically develop both work ties and friendship ties at work, and "You can communicate differently with someone with whom you have work and friendship ties than with whom you just have work ties."

Authenticity is a huge deal. —JACK WELCH

I decided to ask former CEO of General Electric, business guru Jack Welch, why he thinks my approach backfired so badly. He argues that women make a mistake when they try to mimic what they see men do. "Authenticity is a huge deal," he said, for both women and men. "Men are jerks when they're not themselves . . . I mean authenticity is a killer, and women sometimes don't behave as themselves," he says.

For most women, an aggressive verbal style is just out of character. Former Yahoo! CEO Carol Bartz may be the exception. Known for her fearless leadership style as well as her willingness to use foul language, she says, "Well, I mean, listen, this business that goes on about my 'salty language' . . . come on, there are men who could run my language into the ground and nobody cares. Yes, I am an outspoken person; I have been probably for the last twenty years. As I earned the right, I got more outspoken. I just developed a style that works for me, and I think it's authentic. I just met with a lot of the interns, and I said you can't copy me because a) you haven't earned the right, and b) if it's not comfortable, everybody can see that."

For the rest of us who aren't comfortable with it, strong language only backfires. A lot of people I consulted with agree that the problem wasn't really what I said, it was my delivery. I just wasn't being authentic with Phil. But what about the fact that I was authentically angry? Hannah Riley Bowles comments, "Even if you were genuinely pissed, if you were acting like a guy, it probably wouldn't work. There is a lot of evidence, our research included, that adopting the guys' style of doing this is likely to be risky for women. When women just act like the guys, then they pay really important social costs."

Bowles and other researchers have various names for this problem. They call it the double bind, or the backlash effect. Research shows that assertiveness is an important quality for leadership. But when women are assertive, it can hurt them, because being assertive is not an appealing trait in women.

Professors Frank Flynn, Cameron Anderson, and Sebastien Brion tested this effect on a group of business students at New York University. MBA students were asked to read a Harvard Business School case about a very successful Silicon Valley entrepreneur by the name of Heidi Roizen.

The case is often used to teach students networking skills, but the researchers decided to use the case for a study on gender and bias. They gave half their students the case under the real name of Heidi Roizen and the other half a case about "Howard Roizen." The cases were exactly the same, except for a couple of descriptive words: Heidi's "husband" was changed to Howard's "wife," and Heidi the "cheerleader" became Howard the "football player." Both Heidi and Howard were described in assertive terms as take-charge executives, captains of industry.

After reading over the case, the students went online to answer questions about their impressions of Heidi/Howard. They were asked to rate her or him on characteristics such as kindness, generosity, ambition, manipulativeness, concern for others, and a variety of other typically gender-associated traits.

The results were shocking. The students were looking at exactly the same information, but they rated Heidi less kind and less generous than Howard and more power hungry, manipulative, and assertive than Howard. Clearly the students responded negatively to Heidi's aggressiveness.

When the students were asked whether they would want to work with Howard and whether they'd hire Heidi, the researchers discovered that both men and women thought Heidi was competent, but less likeable. Heidi may have been a little full of herself, but Howard was the kind of guy they'd go have a beer with.

The double bind is this: in order to be a competent leader you need to be assertive—but if you're a woman, you're judged harshly for displaying the traits that make you an effective leader.

I wasn't surprised to hear that the data showed men were more critical of women than of other men. But I was surprised that women were equally critical of both genders. Women are as hard on each other as they are on themselves.

Flynn's students insisted that they didn't judge Heidi any differently. After the test was completed, however, Flynn shared the results with them, and they, too, were shocked. Flynn says that confronting this group with their own subconscious bias was a powerful lesson for them all. When Flynn relayed the results to the real Heidi Roizen, she responded, "Well, I guess that's understandable, with a group of grizzled executives." She was as surprised as anyone to learn the test subjects were twenty-six-year-old MBA students.

> *There is a tendency to have a meeting after the meeting, because [women] don't want to say the mean thing in the meeting.* —LIZ BENTLEY

Our Achilles' Heel

The simple fact is that even the most successful women among us just want to be liked.

Executive Coach Liz Bentley has many stories of clients who care too much about how other people feel about them. "A lot of women who are in the workplace right now were raised with the idea of being nice first. You're supposed to be nice. Period. That's the most important quality; if you're described as 'nice' that's a better quality than smart, athletic, competent, and confident. Nice is the most important quality."

Liz has seen this evolve into a very uncomfortable trend in the office. "When [women] are in meetings there is a tendency to have a meeting after the meeting, because they don't want to say the mean thing in the meeting. They don't want to speak. Whereas the guys were never told to be nice; they were told to be smart and confident. So in the meetings they just say what they want to say.

I feel that women have a lot of meetings to talk about what just happened at another meeting. You'll hear, 'What I really want to say' or 'What I really meant to say' . . . that's where I would say women could be more like men. Be a little more direct, a little less emotional, a little less pragmatic, and let go of this false understanding that they have to be nice first."

I think most of us have been in our fair share of "meetings after the meeting." And they waste our time and do nothing to highlight our intelligence to our colleagues.

This need to be liked applies to women from all walks of life—Joy Behar is not comfortable being a bitch. Yes, I said that. Like Susie Essman, Behar rose up the ranks in the world of stand-up comedy. Currently she's on television two hours every weekday, hosting her own talk show as well as *The View*. She is both unfailingly funny and searingly blunt. During the 2008 campaign, Behar famously asked John McCain some of the toughest questions he faced. He arrived on the set of *The View*, no doubt expecting light conversation, when Behar confronted him on his campaign commercials: "We know that those two ads are untrue, they are lies. And yet, you at the end of it say you approve these messages. Do you really approve them?"

This is a woman who doesn't have a hard time speaking her mind, so it might surprise you to learn that she doesn't speak up when it comes to asking for money and perks. "I'm just a big mouth," Behar tells me, "[but] I'm not demanding, and I don't say I have to get special privileges or anything like that." It's not that she doesn't want the big money and the big perks; it's just that, like most women, being demanding makes her uncomfortable. "You want people to feel that you're a team player," she says. "I've always been the good girl, in a certain way. I have always been the good team player."

Plus, there's the risk that she'll be called a bitch. But don't bitches often get what they want? "The squeaky wheel gets the grease, as they say," Behar says. "They don't really give a f—ck that you think that they're a bitch. You and I, we don't like to be thought of as bitches . . . if you don't care that people think you're a bitch, you can run the networks and the country. I don't have that; I'm not comfortable with being a bitch."

Behar is right. I didn't want to be thought of as the b-word. And that was the crux of my problem: I really wanted to be liked.

My desire to be liked outweighed my wish to be valued. When my bosses would compliment me for being "a jack-of-all-trades," a warm feeling rushed over me. I felt . . . liked. But I have learned the hard way that compliments don't pay the bills. Which brings me back to my story, and one of the best and worst moments of my career, all at the same time.

New Hampshire and the Red Hair Clip

New Hampshire was pivotal in the run-up to Super Tuesday back during her first run for the presidency in 2008. This primary would decide whether Hillary Clinton, whose candidacy was on the rocks, would drop her bid for the presidency. Instead it turned out to be the place she "found her voice." But before she did, we found her at 9:30 at night on a high school stage in Nashua. We had been trying to get some time with her all day. My phone did not leave my ear and we did not get out of the car until we nailed down the interview.

Everyone was predicting a crushing loss for Hillary. But the Hillary we saw that night was a winner. As usual, she had been up earlier than everyone and she stayed up later, fighting both the odds and her critics. She was unflappable. Determined. Confident. Hair perfect. Makeup intact.

We walked away from our interview in awe of her physical might and resilience. How was she still going? This is when Joe Scarborough's adoration for "his girlfriend" Hillary Rodham Clinton began. He started to say it every day on the air: "I can't deny it. My girlfriend is tougher than any man I've met on the campaign trail."

She is a force of nature, and clearly when the chips are down, Hillary Clinton is at her very best. To this day, both Joe and I think she was by far the strongest candidate in terms of steel will and political agility. When she won the next day, her surprise victory made for an incredible narrative.

Late into the night, we discussed how impressed we were and what it would mean for the race if she didn't drop out. We were still buzzing about the interview we had worked so hard to get. Joe and I had scrambled across the country by car and by plane and had to be on the air the next morning for another grueling six hours . . . but we didn't care how tired we were. We had the story and a great show to tell it on.

The next day, after the interview aired, my phone rang. I saw it was an NBC line, and I assumed I was going to be given kudos for the Hillary get—maybe I would be closer to getting that raise. They must have heard how hard we worked, how I didn't give up until we got that interview. How we hadn't slept in days but still found a way to nail the story. The interview was aired over and over again on MSNBC and then again on NBC Nightly News. So this must be one of our bosses calling with a pat on the back.

Uh, not quite.

I picked up the phone and heard, "Hello, Mika? What was with that clip in your hair last night? Do not wear that clip again. You looked awful, don't ever wear that clip in your hair again. Seriously, you looked like a cancer survivor. That clip is awful. I am trying to help you here. You can't do it again. I want people to like you."

It's true that when we had caught up with Hillary the night before, Joe and I were both in jeans and winter boots and ragged from days on the road and spending six hours straight on-air each day. I had thrown my hair up in a plastic hair clip that I'd gotten at a drugstore, and my makeup had pretty much worn off. I was beginning to be comfortable traveling with the guys. Just like them, I let the "real me" hang out. When we were under the gun, I simply couldn't look camera-ready at all times. The guys were great and told me not to bother with makeup. That it shouldn't matter so much. That it would be better to show my real side anyway. That is what our show was about. I could be me.

NBC obviously disagreed.

How did I respond to the call?

I apologized.

Again, this is a story of what not to do. Why didn't I simply hang up? That's what Joe would have done. Surely that's what Hillary Clinton would've done! I should have been crystal clear and defiant. I had scored a major victory—that's what the manager should've taken away from that piece. I felt powerful; I was powerful. But I didn't take the opportunity to set her straight.

I'm sure we both would have been better off had I spoken up. We still might not have agreed on the hair clip, but I would have earned her respect, and I would have had the satisfaction of explaining that she'd missed the point: The important thing here was that we'd gotten a key interview on the most exciting night of the election season thus far. This was the stuff of great television.

In the weeks that followed, my exchange with the manager about the damn hair clip stayed with me. Would it have been such a big deal if I'd pushed back? Was I afraid of sounding like a bitch? The answer was probably yes. I realized that wanting to be liked was really getting in my way. But when I took a more aggressive tack and decided that raising my voice would get me somewhere—well, we know how well that worked out. So where was the middle ground? How was I ever going to be both likeable and fairly compensated?

"How women can do both, get what they want materially and also make a positive social image" is a tricky thing to pull off, says Professor Hannah Riley Bowles. "I think it's flawed to say that women need to be trained to negotiate more assertively or that they need more confidence to close the gender gap in negotiation performance." Because clearly, women who are assertive suffer a backlash, so it's entirely reasonable for them to be reticent about asking for what they want.

Bowles tells me that there's no easy solution. Women have to be strategic and come up with their own way of asking for higher pay.

"One strategy that we have found to be effective is what we call using a 'relational account.' This involves explaining why the negotiating request is legitimate in terms that inherently communicate concern for organizational relationships." They have to find a feminine way of getting what they deserve, because negotiating for something like higher compensation in its essence "contradicts what you're supposed to be like as a woman. Giving, not taking; generous, not materialistic . . . it contradicts a lot of expectations we hold for women consciously or unconsciously."

Walking that tightrope of acceptable behavior leaves women in a quandary.

Shelley Zalis, CEO of The Female Quotient, found her voice, and accelerated her career, by following her feminine instincts. She describes how her emphasis on relationships made all the difference.

"I was the only female CEO in the top twenty-five in market research my whole career. I knew that I thought differently. I knew that I had different kinds of ideas, I knew that people and relationships were so important in everything that I did. And I was never recognized for that. I was actually punished for it. In my first review, I was told that I took too much time with clients and I never really understood that.

"I remember saying to my boss, who was a man, 'One day, you will know how wrong you are.' And I had to ask myself. . . . Am I supposed to follow his guidance, that I should sit at my desk to be a great order taker, or should I follow my instincts and continue to spend time developing relationships because that is ultimately how I want to do business?"

I wanted to do business with people that I liked
and I valued and who valued me. —SHELLEY ZALIS

Shelley followed her instincts and continued to work to build strong, loyal relationships with both clients and colleagues. And liking those colleagues was part of the equation. She remembers, "I wanted to do business with people that I liked and I valued and who valued me. I followed my heart and went in that direction. I have had the same clients for over thirty-four years and we go together with everything that we do." When Shelley needed to call on those resources when she sold her research company and started The Female Quotient, those close relationships and her nurturing nature gave her the advantage she needed.

You Have to Put in the Time

Recently I decided to ask Phil about our weird interaction years ago when I tried to act like Joe. He had an interesting take—he emphasized the necessity of building trust.

Phil explains what changed our relationship for the better: "One of the key components to making sure everyone knows your value is putting in the time and developing an honest and meaningful business relationship. A relationship that allows transparency and an ability to speak really openly about how you feel, and sell yourself without the fear of offending the other person. And once you and I developed that—and we did, not long after—we established trust for the better part of our relationship. Now we know each other and we can speak openly to each other."

Phil has seen a real change in me, and presumably himself, now that we've worked together so long and know each other so much better. He tells me, "You're a different person today than you were then. The best thing, I can't emphasize enough, is putting in the time. It's as important in a business relationship as any other relationship. And it's as important for the manager as it is important for the employee."

But how much time and effort are we required to put in to get to know our bosses personally? How much do they really need to know about our personal lives? It's a question we need to consider carefully. We want to be invited to off-site dinners and drinks just like the guys, but in the world we live in now, we have to think about when and where these interactions are appropriate. We have to build these relationships while maintaining professional boundaries to protect ourselves.

My suggestion is, if you're going to spend time with your boss outside the office, do it over lunch or coffee. If you don't already have regular check-ins on your calendar, schedule meetings just to catch up and stay in sync with how the job is going. Not every meeting has to be a tense negotiation. Put yourself out there. A key tenet of knowing your value: If you don't put yourself out there, you never know what can happen.

Downplay, downplay, downplay.
—SHERYL SANDBERG

Facebook COO Sheryl Sandberg agrees that there's a very good reason why women don't own their success: because success and likeability are positively correlated for men and negatively correlated for women. Says Sandberg: "It makes sense that women behave as they do in the workplace. It's not irrational behavior; it's rational behavior not to own our success. That's the point. It would be easier if the answer were to tell everyone just to start negotiating more. But it's not so easy, because it's not necessarily going to work. Just like what happened to you, it backfires."

Sandberg's two children were both young when I first interviewed her in 2010, and when I ask her how she handles the dual roles of motherhood and executive, she says, "I'll tell you what I always say: I do everything badly. No man ever says that, by the way, that's what we say." (In fact, as Sandberg and I talk further about work-life balance, I exclaim, "You're amazing!" Her automatic response: "I'm really not." She's nothing if not consistent.)

Sandberg's guiding principle for successful women: "Downplay, downplay, downplay."

But then the question is, if women have to continually downplay their success, if they aren't aggressive about getting paid what they're worth, how do they get anywhere? Obviously there have to be times when you don't soft-pedal your success, when you need to step up and be heard. Again, we have to find our own path.

And if anyone knows about forging her own path, it is Sheryl. Inspired by a TED Talk she gave in 2010, she wrote *Lean In: Women, Work, and the Will to Lead,* which has become a fixture for women looking to advance their careers. It became a rallying cry for women all over the world. And since the first edition of *Know Your Value,* Sheryl tragically lost her husband, Dave Goldberg, in 2015. But like the superhero that she has always been, she turned that devastation and grief into a platform to help other women. She wrote *Option B: Facing Adversity, Building Resilience, and Finding Joy* and has shown women another way to "lean in"—leaning in to their grief.

Finding your own path is exactly the advice Donny Deutsch gives me when I bemoan the fact that women are punished both for being too aggressive and for not being aggressive enough: "I think there's a middle ground," he says. "I think it's about being smart. The answer is understanding those two sides of the coin. Saying I'm going to be firm, I'm going to be direct, I'm still managing up to a weaker sex, women managing men, in order to get what I want. I'm not going to challenge them to a duel, but I'm not going to be passive and I'm not going to use 'please' and 'thank you' and all that stuff. It's doing it with a softer touch, but with that same level of firepower, and that's the difference."

Finding the Middle Ground: Not Too Soft, Not Too Hard

The experiences of women in male-dominated industries illustrate on a larger scale the hurdles women face every day. When I met Sheila Bair, former chair of the FDIC, for a sit-down interview for this book, my stomach was in knots. In 2009, *Forbes* named Bair the second most powerful woman in the world for the role she played in handling the financial crisis. I wondered if a woman who was dealing with the momentous problems facing our economy on a regular basis would be able to relate at all to my career issues. I was stunned at how much we had in common. Soon we were chuckling together over the similarities of our struggles, despite the difference in our fields.

Don't ever get emotional. —SHEILA BAIR

I ask Bair to give examples of the strategies she uses to make her way through the male bastion of finance.

"Emotionalism doesn't work," Bair tells me. "Don't ever get emotional. Sometimes that's hard. You get so frustrated and you care deeply. I'm the kind of person who cares deeply, but emotionalism never works. It always has the opposite effect."

I ask, "Did you ever get emotional?"

"There were probably a couple of times during the bailout discussions . . ." Bair answers.

"Are we talking about tears?" I ask.

"No, it never got that far," she says. "I'm really talking more about anger; for me it was more anger. When you're angry it hurts your ability to think straight. If you start to get angry, the adrenaline starts pumping in you."

"If no one is listening to you, how do you not get angry?" I ask.

"Frankly, I think that just takes a lot of maturity to deal with, and I've gotten better at it over the years. You just have to control yourself. If you let yourself respond with anger or with emotion, it's going to make things worse, not better, and you'll suffer a loss of respect."

"Can a man get angry?" I ask.

"Yes, and they even get angry with each other," Bair says, "and it doesn't seem to do anything at all. But if we get angry with them it doesn't work, it backfires. I've witnessed men at my level go at each other on occasion, and that's just accepted, even by the press." If she had growled in a similar way, she would've been labeled an emotional woman.

I ask Bair if being too assertive has backfired for her, the way it did for me when I tried to get a raise.

"With certain personalities, yes, it can," she answers. "I think it's unfortunate that sometimes being assertive doesn't work, where being helpless works or being flattering works. I say that because I try to be a good person and not a disingenuous person, but I recognize that certain strategies work. I think sometimes it makes them feel they're in control; I'm sorry—it does. It prevents them from feeling threatened by your argument if you're coming to them for help: 'I have this idea. Advise me how we can move this forward. Is this a good idea?' You know, sometimes that approach works better. It does. It can be disarming in a way that produces results without being threatening."

That's right. The former chairman of the FDIC suggests flattery. I was both surprised and amused.

And I suspect many women reading this may roll their eyes. But I went on to hear the same advice from women as different as Carol Bartz and Susie Essman.

Former Yahoo! CEO Carol Bartz agrees that the best way to get men to listen is to compliment them. She tells me about an economic summit she was invited to when Bill Clinton was running for president. She claims that she was invited "because, you know, they had to have so many skirts," but then she was promptly ignored. "I walked in and nobody would pay any attention to me. They would shake my hand and be looking over my shoulder, obviously trying to see if there was somebody much more important behind me. I found that I finally had to start by saying, 'Oh, I've always admired you so much,' you know . . . blah, blah, blah, even to be able to engage with any of the men."

Basically, Bartz tells me, "You just do what you have to, to fit in."

Comedian and actress Susie Essman tells me that one of the advantages that women have over men is that we have better people skills. We don't need to be aggressive, because we have methods of manipulation that are far more effective. "One of my strategies is always to play to men's narcissism in a way that is so subtle they don't know what hit them. I think we have to use our wiles," she says. "When I say feminine wiles, I don't mean sexual. I mean . . . we're a completely different species, men and women. I think that we have to recognize those differences. I do believe that women are—I don't want to say smarter— but we're more well-rounded. There are all these articles they're writing now about how women are better CEOs than men because they're more conciliatory. In life it's worked really well for me to be really conciliatory but strong at the same time. It's a balance. We are fence menders. We build relationships and building relationships is the way to go."

A number of women I interviewed agreed that flattery is the way to go, but not necessarily flirting. They're not the same thing. If the person on the receiving end is a man, however, being complimentary may be interpreted as flirting. Hannah Riley Bowles warns that "The data out on flirting—research done by Laura Kray at UC Berkeley—is not that encouraging. Flirting tends to make you appealing, but not particularly persuasive." So here again, women have to walk a very fine line.

Hard as Nails, Warm as Toast

Women's advocate Marie C. Wilson echoed what others have said: When women play hardball and negotiate like a man, they just don't get the same response that a man would. She says the people who teach negotiation, like Professor Linda Babcock at Carnegie Mellon, observe that when women go in to negotiate, they have to do it by being "relentlessly pleasant." We still carry our own stereotypes about what women are supposed to be like, and yet when you go in to negotiate for a raise, "It's hard to remember that as a woman you have to go negotiate with a big smile on your face," she says.

There really are different expectations for behavior. Does Wilson envision a time when women won't have to negotiate differently than men? Yes. Wilson believes all of that will change when the numbers shift, and women outnumber men in the workplace—or at least surpass that magic one-third.

"But until that happens, women walk a fine line," Wilson says. "Because, as my friend Anna Quindlen says, women 'have to be tough as nails and warm as toast.' . . . You get penalized when you take either one of those positions separately. If you go in and you're apologetic, you know, you're toast. If you go in and you do it in a way that's tough as nails, then you're hammered. You have to go in and do it in a way that is relentlessly pleasant."

Many of the people I spoke with believe that more women are in positions of power, and if more people (both men and women) are made aware of their own unconscious biases, that women will be able to be assertive in the workplace with fewer repercussions. Until then, we figure it out as we go.

Huffington Post and Thrive cofounder Arianna Huffington knows very well the potential social risk of being a powerful woman. "The most important thing for women is not to internalize the attacks on them, and to realize that any time they speak out they are going to have attacks leveled at them," she advises. "Let's face it: Our culture still isn't comfortable with outspoken women. As Marlo Thomas famously put it, 'A man has to be Joe McCarthy to be called ruthless. All a woman has to do is put you on hold.'" Huffington says that she finds the best way to neutralize this kind of attitude is through humor and perspective.

"Too often in our culture, strong women get stereotyped as ball-busters, which is as insulting as it is ludicrous," Huffington tells me. "In my experience, the strongest, most fearless women I know are also the most creative and productive—and the ones who most want to support other women. And, honestly, wouldn't any healthy man really prefer to be involved with a woman—either personally or professionally—who is driven by her true thoughts, feelings, beliefs, and desires instead of her fears?"

In my experience, the strongest, most fearless women I know are also the most creative and productive—and the ones who most want to support other women. —ARIANNA HUFFINGTON

The fact is, there just aren't enough female role models. As Hannah Riley Bowles points out, "The high-powered female executive is really a new phenomenon, and these women are creating what that person is as they're doing it." Men have plenty of role models when they're looking for examples of people in the highest leadership positions. "Women do have to come up with their own ways of doing these things," she says.

So if acting like a man didn't get me anywhere, what strategies should I have used instead?

CHAPTER 5

WHAT MEN KNOW

We Can't Act Like Them,
but We Can Learn from Them

My story, with Chrystia Freeland, Arianna Huffington, Kate White,
Elizabeth Warren, Suze Orman, Sheila Bair, Donny Deutsch, Valerie Jarrett,
Carol Bartz, Brooksley Born, Liz Bentley, and Jack Welch

Finding Our Own Way

My own experience, and now the experiences shared by so many other
women in these pages, convinces me that women can't act like men
and expect to be liked, to be able to lead, and to be paid what they're
worth. But we still need to accomplish all of those goals. Former global
editor-at-large of Reuters and current Minister of Foreign Affairs in
Canada since January 2017 Chrystia Freeland notes, "We as women are
still immigrants; we don't speak the native language very well. It might

not be that these male ways of behaving are, absent other factors, better, but they are the dominant cultural mode, and like all immigrants we have to conform to the dominant cultural mode. We can learn a lot from the men around us."

Surely our demeanor and delivery have to be different, and that's our main challenge. *Huffington Post* cofounder Arianna Huffington describes the situation succinctly: "In order to conquer the workplace as women, we need to approach it in our own unique way, not as carbon copies of men: briefcase-carrying, pinstripe-wearing career machines who just happen to have vaginas." The way to get ahead? Huffington answers, "By learning how to play the men's office 'game,' but tailoring it to our own style."

A Sense of Entitlement

In addition to a career as the author of best-selling mysteries and thrillers such as *Hush* as well as nonfiction books such as *Why Good Girls Don't Get Ahead but Gutsy Girls Do*, Kate White is the former editor-in-chief of *Cosmopolitan* magazine. She has many stories to tell about what women in the workplace could learn from men.

> *Some of the guys I've worked with have just had a really great sense of entitlement.* —KATE WHITE

When she was the editor of *Working Woman* magazine, White hired a guy—let's call him Jack—as a senior editor. There were three other senior editors, all women. When Jack was first hired, all the editors had their own offices, but soon, for economic reasons, the magazine moved into a new building with less space. "It turned out that all four senior editors were going to have to work out of this big room that had once been the company library," she says. White knew this would not go over well. "I went down to see what was happening, and discovered that Jack had slipped some money to the movers when all the furniture was being delivered," she tells me. "He arranged for them to give him a big old bookcase, which he used to divide off his area, and then he got them to bring up a little couch from the basement. Brilliant. Suddenly he had an office. If you had walked in you would have thought he was the boss and the three women were in the typing pool. He just said to himself, 'Okay, this isn't the best situation. What do I have to do to fix it to my advantage?'"

White says many women think, "'Hey, we're following orders here, we're doing what we're supposed to do,' whereas a lot of guys in the workplace make up the rules as they go along. Men scam the situation . . . Jack had an air of entitlement that said, 'I deserve this, and I'm going to get it.' I just laughed and thought, 'What can I learn from this guy?'"

She's right; a woman's tendency is to fall in line and accept the status quo, even if it doesn't benefit her. Women seem more willing to be accommodating than to insist on being accommodated.

> *Someone needs to do this. Someone needs to mop the floor.*
> *Okay, hand me the mop.* —ELIZABETH WARREN

Morning Joe regular guest United States Senator Elizabeth Warren (D-MA) is a former Harvard law professor. In September 2010 she was appointed assistant to the president and special advisor to the secretary of the treasury on the Consumer Financial Protection Bureau, a position in which she built the new agency that will oversee the rules on financial products such as mortgages and credit cards. Since the original publication of *Know Your Value*, Elizabeth Warren successfully ran for the United States Senate and has become a champion for women on the world's stage. Today, Warren is considered a viable presidential candidate for Democrats in 2020 and is—albeit accidentally—the inspiration for the new feminist rally cry, "Nevertheless, she persisted."

She is a woman who surely would be horrified by all the mistakes I've made along the way in my career—or so I thought.

As a longtime advocate for consumers, Warren has gone up against some of the biggest names on Wall Street, and she has famously locked horns with then Treasury Secretary Tim Geithner. Warren, who has been on *Time* magazine's list of the World's Most Influential People for two years running and often appears on our show to talk about the economy and financial reform, impresses me as a sharp, gutsy, no-nonsense woman. But she admits to me that when it comes to her personal value in the workplace, she still struggles.

Warren remembers how surprised she was when she realized her male colleagues had that sense of entitlement that she lacked. It happened when she first started teaching at the University of Houston. Before the semester began, she heard from the associate dean, who was scheduling courses. "I got the call asking, 'Would you teach the lousy course at the lousy hour on the lousy day in the lousy room?'" she says. She didn't want to teach that particular class, but she didn't see any way around it: "I thought, I'm sure someone needs to teach at the lousy hour on the lousy day in the lousy room, so I said, 'I'll do it.'"

A couple of years later, Warren was promoted to associate dean, and it was now her job to assign courses, classrooms, and time slots. "So I took the map from the year before and started laying it out, and I sent all these notes out on what and when I needed people to teach," she remembers. "But every single man on the faculty who didn't like their schedule sent me back an e-mail saying, 'You know, you don't understand, I only teach at ten o'clock on Mondays, Tuesdays, and Wednesdays.'"

And the women?

Warren says, "Every single woman could be leveraged into teaching the lousy course at the lousy time in the lousy room. Men would just say, 'No. That's not convenient for me.' I thought, 'This is astonishing!'"

I ask Warren, "It never crossed your mind to say no?"

"Never," Warren says.

"Why?"

"Partly I felt lucky to be there; partly, I'm the cooperator, you know, 'let's get the job done.' Someone needs to do this. Someone needs to mop the floor. Okay, hand me the mop. I really see this as the difference between putting ourselves, if not first, at least putting equivalent value on ourselves . . . we don't see our own worth. We see how we can be helpful to the team or to the group. We see what we can add without stopping to ask, 'Wait a minute, this is a valuable contribution—why am I making this, and what am I getting in return for it?'

"You're always careful about generalizations here, but for me it doesn't even cross my mind until later, when I'm committed to do something and I suddenly look around and realize, 'So how come the three people who agreed to do the hard, invisible labor here are all women?'"

Warren points out that while the low-profile jobs may be both necessary and important, they just don't garner the accolades or the money and promotions. For that reason, men simply never pick up the mop. She saw this at her faculty meetings at Harvard. "Someone will say, 'Well, you know we should hire X because he . . .' and they will name three very visible accomplishments. And I know for a fact, and every woman in the room knows for a fact, that X is a real pain in the rear: X won't cooperate, won't help out, won't be a team player. X will not help move the whole institution forward, and that's regarded as irrelevant. You know, it's the difference between the big, valuable things that people do, and all that stuff that women do—that's all that crap stuff. That's the stuff no one notices, no one cares. No one values."

I can think of countless lousy shifts that I've volunteered to work in my life. Time away from my husband and my kids, time that I needed to take care of myself, that I gave up in order to work. To be the cooperator, the person with the mop. I know for a fact those lost hours made no difference to my employers, but it is the lost time with my family that I'll never get back. I often pushed myself to extremes to get nothing in return except bad health, and at one point, a baby with a broken leg. Warren's description of herself when she was starting out made me cringe, because that was me. Always trying to run faster, to please everyone, and very seldom getting anything in return.

If You're Not Paid for It, Don't Do It

Personal-finance expert and force of nature Suze Orman argues that for their own sake, women have to resist the urge to always pick up the mop. When you know what you're worth, you'll have an easier time asking to be compensated for what you're bringing to the job. And if you're not getting paid for it, take a lesson from men and don't do it.

"I know my own worth and I'm not going to settle for less," Orman says. "It's really just that simple. When I'm giving my speaking lectures, I get exactly what I want for my speaking lectures, and if you can't pay me, then I'm not going to speak for you. I get exactly what I want from CNBC, and I'm very happy. I don't have to demand; you either give it to me or you don't. If you don't, then it's not my problem."

Of course, at this point in her career, it's easy for Suze Orman to say no. She acknowledges that in times of recession, most people don't have that luxury. Most people do what they have to do, and sometimes, that does include picking up the mop and even working for free. "When you're first working for someone, your goal is to make those people whom you are dependent on dependent on you," Orman advises. "So when you first start working, you do not demand anything, you do not ask for anything. That's when you do everything you can, even if you're not asked to do it. You make them totally dependent on you—and then you've reversed the power." When you really need the money, or the opportunity, sometimes you do have to get your foot in the door and take the lousy shift. But once you've made yourself essential, that's when you have leverage. It's up to you to make sure your boss sees your contribution and knows you expect to be paid for it.

Orman says she sometimes worked for free as she worked her way up. She worked unpaid the entire first year of her show, because she and her managers weren't able to settle on contract terms. But at the end of the first year she had proven herself and was in an excellent negotiating position.

Be Visible—and Willing to Promote Yourself

Former FDIC chair Sheila Bair told me that while she hasn't haggled over the issue of compensation, she has certainly felt at times that her opinions have not been valued: "Traditionally women's work or opinions or both have not been valued as much as they should. The societal notion that women's work or opinions are less valuable can seep into our own thinking. Perhaps on a subconscious level, but I think it does seep in. We can be accepting of what we get and not ask for more and not think that we deserve more. I think that goes from compensation, office space, titles, to getting credit for saying something and making it your idea. Somehow it's a bad thing to stand up for yourself or promote yourself . . . to speak up and say, 'I deserve to be paid X,' and we feel embarrassed or ashamed or bashful about that, and we shouldn't."

> *The societal notion that women's work or opinions*
> *are less valuable can seep into our own thinking.*
> **—SHEILA BAIR**

Bair told me she thinks women need to be more assertive. She says we need to educate our managers about our worth: "When there is unequal treatment, learn how to promote yourself in a way that is constructive. You don't have to be obnoxious about it; you can be factual about it. You say, 'This is my idea,' and don't back down. Say it, and don't be embarrassed by saying it."

Advertising exec Donny Deutsch says that for men, keeping track of accomplishments is as natural as breathing. "Men grow up playing games and keeping score from the time they're four years old, and that continues in the workplace. Keeping score by tracking how much money you make, how big your office is, what are the perks, what do other people think, how does it look."

Deutsch says all that scorekeeping makes male employees high maintenance. "I've found without exception that for every alpha male who has worked for me, I've had to spend a lot more time negotiating literally and figuratively . . . the size of everything. For them it's, 'I want more; what's in it for me?'"

Women may not need or want to keep calling attention to themselves, but as Obama advisor Valerie Jarrett put it, "If you're not negotiating the size of everything, odds are, you're not going to become the boss." Because as I pointed out, even if we don't care about nice offices or elevated titles, the rest of the world does recognize those symbolic, status-oriented achievements.

Being Visible Has Its Drawbacks, but So What?

News of Carol Bartz's compensation was splashed across the front pages of newspapers across the country when she got the job as Yahoo! CEO in 2009. Bartz says she found it "absolutely fascinating" how reports exaggerated her pay, calling her "'the highest-paid whatever,' which is such bullshit because if they really read the fine print, they'd see the stock price has to go up, the moon has to be full, and cats have to howl and so forth," before she'd get her full compensation package.

First I got mad, and then I got embarrassed, and then I said,
*"You know what? Not my problem." —*CAROL BARTZ

But what bothered her most was "the sheer embarrassment of the scrutiny." Everyone was coming up to my husband and saying, 'Well, I guess you can afford a new set of clubs,' and, you know, razzing him. People were putting copies of articles in his locker. It was just bizarre. First I got mad, and then I got embarrassed, and then I said, 'You know what? Not my problem.' I'm proud of this, and if some young woman thinks she can be 'the highest-paid whatever,' then good!"

Why are we afraid to be called self-promoting, and why wouldn't we feel great about being "the highest-paid whatever"? Maybe we feel as if we're being set up to be knocked down or that people think we're only in it for the money. Or maybe the fact that people notice that we're highlighting our accomplishments distracts from the accomplishments themselves?

In her experience as a law professor and in her government positions as chairwoman of TARP and the chief advisor in charge of setting up the Consumer Financial Protection Bureau, Elizabeth Warren knows that to be labeled self-promoting may not be a bad thing for a man, but it is for a woman: "It's like having something sort of deeply wrong about you. You sense this is a really bad thing."

The notion that I'm self-promoting somehow
makes me gasp. —ELIZABETH WARREN

Warren has spent years advocating for consumer protections in the financial-services industry, and she was often interviewed by reporters covering the financial crisis. She has taken a lot of flak from those who don't like her views, and she told me she understood that that came with the territory. But when the *Wall Street Journal* called her "self-promoting," she says that she felt transported back to her childhood in Oklahoma, suddenly feeling like an odd girl out. She remembers thinking, "'Oh my god, I do so much less press than I'm asked to do, and when I do it I always try to do it in the service of trying to teach something, trying to advance an idea' . . . it really stung."

Warren continues: "You know, when someone says, 'Oh, she's just plain stupid,' it doesn't cut to the quick. It doesn't undermine me in the same way. It doesn't even throw me off. But the notion that I'm self-promoting somehow makes me gasp." She says that finally, after several years of working in a much more public position, she's developed thicker skin and the ability to stop and think, "'Wait a minute. Why does *that* one cut to the quick?' I think more than once I've wondered, 'Would you say that if I were a man?'"

Speak Up, and Make Sure Your Ideas Are Heard

"I've been in a room countless times where I said something and no one responded, no one paid attention. Then a man has said the exact same thing, and people have listened," Valerie Jarrett tells me. "It hasn't happened to me in this White House, but it's happened to me countless times in the past. I think that every woman has experienced that. I don't know whether it's the way we speak it, or if it's because we're women and people have discounted what we said. I can think of many, many times when I've said something and it's been overlooked."

Study after study has documented this phenomenon. And woman after woman told me she had experienced some version of the same scenario. But for women to achieve their value, they have to find a way to be heard. Nowhere has that been more difficult and more public than on Wall Street, where a few women have dared to go up against an army of powerful men.

What was frustrating was that they wouldn't even engage. —SHEILA BAIR

96

Former FDIC chair Sheila Bair was one of the first people to raise concerns about problems with the subprime mortgage market. She famously battled the "men in charge" of the various regulatory agencies. She tells me it was often difficult to get her counterparts to listen. It was probably for a variety of reasons, including the FDIC's traditionally conservative philosophy and posture. "I become frustrated when people won't even engage," she says. "If you're not going to agree with me, tell me why you don't agree with me and let me respond to that. Don't just nod and smile and go off and don't do anything. So that's really frustrating, and I think that's the first hurdle: at least getting people to engage—even if they're going to disagree with you or not accept your views, at least get them to listen and have a give and take. You have to keep coming back at them and demand a response to your views."

When I press Bair for an instance she would be willing to share in which she felt her ideas were ignored, she refers me to a series of public incidents in 2007. At the time, the mortgage market was starting to go south, and Bair was pushing for a federal program that would encourage banks to modify loans for millions of homeowners. The idea was to lower payments and extend the length of the mortgages so families could remain in their homes, keep the mortgages performing, and head off an epidemic of foreclosures.

Bair was initially unable to convince Treasury Secretary Hank Paulson or the Bush White House to support the program. But then Governor Arnold Schwarzenegger decided to launch a loan modification project in California modeled on her plan. When Schwarzenegger adopted the project, he gave the idea additional credibility, and Hank Paulson saw its merits. "He came around . . . and it provided some momentum for the administration to say, 'Okay, if Arnold is doing it, it must be a good idea.' So then we did it on a federal level."

Like Brooksley Born and Sheila Bair, Elizabeth Warren talks about the "profound insularity on Wall Street." She says, "The guys who ran it were guys who talked only to each other and valued only each other. That was their downfall. They didn't want to hear the evidence that said, 'Your game doesn't work. Your plan is broken' . . . and so it was, you know, 'Lalalala, we can't hear you.'"

I've picked the girls' end of the discussion.
—ELIZABETH WARREN

Warren's work had an effect on Wall Street and corporate America. She told me that she works in "a field in which male voices dominate almost exclusively."

Warren says she was not just in the minority because she's a woman, but also because she has taken the "girls' side" of finance: "I want to talk about the consumer impact of much of what Wall Street does, and in many circles that makes it doubly unpopular. You know, I've picked the girls' end of the discussion . . . because the cool stuff, the guys' stuff, is to talk about leveraged buyouts and credit-default swaps.

"I've been in groups of academics and we're talking about financial innovation, and everyone in the room wanted to talk about [mortgage-backed securities and collateralized debt obligations], and when I would raise my hand to say, 'The first problem with financial innovation has been the families . . . the thirty-page credit card agreements and mortgages' . . . there's just a long dead silence, and finally someone says, 'Well, yes, but we only talk about the things that have a really important impact.'

"I know what all that means and I can talk about it. We can sit here and have back-and-forth on theoretical ideas and what the data show, but the part that has been missing from the conversation is the impact on families . . . that the raw materials for much of the financial bubble and crash were people's home mortgages and credit card agreements. We know that now, but no one wanted to talk about this on the eve of the Great Recession."

If I respect you, I will disagree with you.
If I don't respect you, I'll just say you don't understand.
—ELIZABETH WARREN

Despite resistance, Warren continued to voice her concerns. And she suffered a backlash, in a very public way.

She remembers the litany: "'Doesn't have the right background, doesn't play the political game, doesn't understand how things are done' . . . for which there's a little voice in me that always said, 'Oh, no, I understand; I just think it's wrong.' . . . The whole game is 'doesn't understand' rather than 'we just disagree.' You know, people need to show respect to disagree with you: If I respect you, I will disagree with you. If I don't respect you, I'll just say you don't understand."

How many men are called strident?
—BROOKSLEY BORN

Perhaps the best example of this backlash came a decade before the economy faltered, when another female regulator, Brooksley Born, went up against Wall Street. Born was the chair of the Commodity Futures Trading Commission (CFTC). In the late 1990s, she warned of the risk from the credit default swaps and other financial time bombs that would eventually cause the economic collapse. But nobody listened.

Born's agency wanted to regulate these financial instruments, and that made some very powerful men angry. Born recalls, "They said I was pressing it. Well, I believed it. I thought that the country was in danger. I thought that the American public was going to suffer if we didn't do something."

She was publicly pilloried as being "difficult," "stubborn," and "strident."

Born says that she had to ignore those labels. "If you stick to your guns, we all know that a woman behaving the way a man would is described by a different adjective," she tells me. "But when it's important, it's important to do more to be heard." Now, years later, she can laugh about her own bad press, but she asks, "I mean, how many men are called strident?"

Still, Born never backed down, and was eventually rewarded for her tenacity by being forced out of her job by then–Federal Reserve Chairman Alan Greenspan and Treasury Secretary Robert Rubin.

So What Do You Do When You're Being Ignored?

Sheila Bair insists, "Don't be embarrassed about sticking up for yourself and proposing good ideas. Try and carry the day at meetings, and if someone else tries to poach [your ideas], stand up for yourself and say, 'Well, that's exactly what I just said.' You can do that politely—you don't have to be confrontational."

Carol Bartz, however, is happy to be confrontational. When this happens to her, she tells me, "I say, 'I think I just said that about ten minutes ago.' I do that. Come on, they are not going to get away with that shit. I say, 'I said that ten minutes ago. What was it about the way I said it that didn't really work for you guys?' You have to do that. There's nothing wrong with that—it's a perfectly legitimate question."

Bartz points out that men will also use the passive-aggressive tactic of not responding at all. "You know, where they seem to agree but they really don't," she says. "I've always said, if you have an opinion, I don't care what it is, we have a starting point. Which means I can convince you differently and you can convince me differently. But if I don't know what you're thinking and then you leave and I think you think one thing and you never did, we will never get anything done."

Elizabeth Warren says what has worked best for her is "to let the men talk, but then to say, 'Yes, but let me ask that question again . . . maybe I didn't quite hear the answer, but let me push on that again,' because it means I'm listening, I'm treating this as a two-way conversation, and I have noticed that you danced away from the central point. . . . For me that's always been the most effective."

But former GE CEO Jack Welch argues that women don't have to do anything to be heard: "When we're in a meeting and a woman speaks up—because they don't often speak up—when they do you can hear a pin drop."

I think he's probably right in situations where there's only one or two women: you stand out by virtue of being the only one of your kind. But more often than not, women have to try harder to be heard.

All the tools mentioned here add up to one piece of advice: Be confident enough to raise your hand. Men just seem to have an easier time doing it, but making yourself visible is no less important for women. Bringing attention to yourself, your ideas, and your achievements means you'll be scrutinized. And if you fail, people will ask whether any woman can handle the job. But it's hard to get ahead if you're invisible.

Personally, I can use each one of these pieces of advice on the set of *Morning Joe*, and I work every day to keep them in mind.

CHAPTER 6

AT THE BARGAINING TABLE

Table Manners and Tactical Maneuvers

My story, with Suze Orman, Carol Bartz, Lesley Jane Seymour,
Kate White, Arianna Huffington, Donny Deutsch, Valerie Jarrett,
Tina Brown, Hannah Riley Bowles, Carol Smith, Nora Ephron,
Frank Flynn, Jack Welch, JJ Ramberg, and Joy Behar

Negotiate Like a Powerful Woman

Personal finance expert Suze Orman says the reason my attempts to get a raise failed is that I didn't know how to "negotiate like a powerful woman." I should have done my homework and come to the table armed with information and alternatives, not just a catalog of emotions and self-doubt. "The problem is that fear of failure comes when you haven't properly prepared for success," she says. "I am sure that you went in to negotiate your salary from a place of fear, and fear is one of the main internal obstacles to wealth."

What follows is a wealth of advice from a variety of women (and men) about what to do (and not do) when you're asking for a raise or negotiating a job offer.

Know Your Contributions and Their Market Value

In her book *Women & Money: Owning the Power to Control Your Destiny*, Suze Orman gives detailed advice to women about how to protect themselves financially and get the money they deserve. She orders women who want a raise to be prepared. First, document your achievements, and put together a list of all the ways you have met and exceeded expectations. Then, "Tell your boss you want to set up a meeting to discuss your compensation. Prior to that meeting, you are to give your boss a one-page outline of your achievements. Not ten pages—one page. The idea is that you are stating in clear terms what value you have brought to the company and why now is the time for the company to show that it values your effort."

The fact that you deserve a raise or haven't had one in years is not a persuasive argument. What makes a persuasive argument are solid facts and figures about what you've done and what other people, with the same skills and experience and accomplishments, are making for the same job.

Let me say it again: You are not prepared unless you know the market value of your contributions. I can't stress this enough. Why is it such a big secret? Seriously. What are you worth? What I've learned is, you should constantly be asking people about salary. Really wrap your arms around what work is worth what. The more you talk to people and the closer you get to them, the more they will tell you. Go ahead—ask. At this point I pretty much know what everybody is getting paid at MSNBC, and I think that's part of my job, in terms of knowing my value.

For decades, companies have prohibited their employees from sharing information about their wages. In January 2009, Congress introduced the Paycheck Fairness Act, which was intended to ensure that women get paid as well as men for equal work. But the legislation, which would have made it easier for women to sue employers who pay them less than men and made it illegal for employers to retaliate against workers who shared information about wage practices, was defeated by the Senate in November 2010.

Even if you're prohibited from asking your colleagues directly about their own salaries, general information about salary ranges is widely available. This is the value of interviewing at other companies and maintaining contacts across your industry. I encourage people to talk—not just to other women in your field, who may be making less just like you, but to men as well. You can ask what people think the range is for a certain position, or what they think you should be making without directly asking about their salary or telling them yours. Over time, by asking and googling salary ranges from a variety of sources, you really can learn the market rate for certain positions. I know what local anchors make compared with what network anchors make, what anchors make compared with what reporters make. Naturally every case is different, but you can get a sense of the ballpark you should be playing in.

If you're in an industry that uses them, headhunters and agents can be a great resource on the subject of fair market value. Because headhunters fill positions at a variety of levels, and because agents represent more than one person, they should be able to fill you in on what others make—or at least give you that ballpark. And if they're giving you bad information, they are not good at what they do. It's their job to be in the know. So utilize them wisely. Don't just wait for the phone to ring, and for someone to volunteer to pay you market rate for your work. Do your research, and thoroughly understand your leverage.

But it's also just kind of instinctive. I mean, seriously. I signed a contract that I intuitively knew was not right. I knew that I was worth more. But I let fear, and the potential of being disliked, supersede my instincts.

When I started at MSNBC again, as a freelancer, I knew what I signed up for. I had no complaints about that. And by the way, punching in and punching out at the same time every day—to me that was worth my making a lot less. That was fine. But when I started on *Morning Joe*, when I started to become part of a brand of two people, Joe and Mika, or when we became a team of Joe, Mika, and Willie, then we were a commodity. I knew what they were making, and yet I accepted less. I would love to believe that I'm alone in that stupidity. But I fear I'm one of many.

Researchers say part of the reason why women don't know what their peers are earning is social norms. They may not feel that discussing money is appropriate, because making a ton of money fulfills a masculine ideal, not a feminine one. Despite the fact that we've been in the workforce for generations, the cultural ideal of women as caregivers hasn't shifted. Women are still expected to be more selfless than men, so even talking about money—let alone asking for it—makes us uncomfortable.

Carol Bartz says that while women will compare themselves with their colleagues, "the women don't always find out as easily what everybody else makes. The men seem to find out somehow. And I don't know why that is."

These days it's easier than ever to find out what people make. Employees share salary information on websites such as Vault.com and Glassdoor.com; sites like Payscale.com and Salary.com can give you an idea of salaries for comparative positions in your geographic area. But nothing beats talking with people.

Former *More* magazine editor-in-chief and founder of CoveyClub, Lesley Jane Seymour says, "A big problem with women is that they go in not having done their homework; they don't know what everybody else is making. . . . If you do your homework, then you walk in and you present your facts and you can say, 'Here's what other people in this company at the same level are paid. Let me show you all the facts and figures.'" Seymour doesn't think it's easy for anyone to ask for a raise, even men, because in that situation you feel like a child asking for their allowance. Everybody struggles. Again, "the key is to do your research. The most important thing that people don't realize, especially women, is you can't go in there expecting people to take care of you and that they're going to be fair. They're going to try to get the best deal they can."

Host of MSNBC's *Your Business*, JJ Ramberg, knows this to be true. "When I went in to ask for a raise, I went in heavily armed with data. I had a stack of papers backing up what I was asking for. And so my advice is, if you feel uncomfortable with what you're asking for, or if you feel like somebody might not think you deserve it, or if you feel like you're being pushy, or any of those things that historically women have felt when they're going in, then back yourself up with data."

When You're Asking for a Raise, Pick Your Moment

Author and former editor of *Cosmopolitan*, Kate White, offers some advice about timing: "Often women wait to deal with their raise when it's announced to them, but by that time it's already etched into the budget. You need to go in a month or so before you know they're going to start giving the raises and just say, 'Look, I know you're probably planning the budget, and I'd just like an opportunity to tell you how much my job has expanded this year, and I hope my raise can reflect this.'"

And Then, Just Do It

If you're prepared—you've documented your achievements and you know the fair market value of your work—it should be easier to take the emotion out of asking for a raise. Your compensation is no longer about you, it's about the facts in front of you.

The Huffington Post's Arianna Huffington urges women to be fearless: "Really, what's the worst that can happen? We are told no, and we're no worse off than we were before. Just look around and you'll see plenty of evidence that asking for what we want results not in the realization of our worst fears but in getting what we want."

Ultimately, as Donny Deutsch says, "You have to ask for it, and that's that."

Here's another thing to remember: When you realize that every raise you'll get in the future is a percentage of what you're already making, if you don't push to make more money right now, the cumulative effect a few years down the line will be enormous.

> *You stand in front of that mirror*
> *and you practice until you are confident.*
> *You go in there and you be an actress.*
> —CAROL BARTZ

Whether you're accepting an offer or asking for a raise, ask for more money with confidence. And if you don't have it, fake it. Carol Bartz tells me a story about a female friend of hers. "[She] was after a senior position in a company, and she knew she was a finalist and a guy was the other finalist. She was expecting a salary of $90,000 and maybe 2,000 shares of stock or something like that. She found out that this guy was asking $125,000 and 2,000 in stock. And she called me, and she said, 'What should I do?'"

Bartz instructed her friend to march in and tell them that she wanted $125,000 and the stock too, but she balked. "She said, 'Oh, I can't do that. I couldn't keep a straight face.'"

Bartz tells me her friend honestly felt that she wouldn't have to tout her value, that it was obvious. But Bartz insisted: "I said, 'You stand in front of that mirror and you practice until you are confident. You go in there and you be an actress.'"

Bartz's friend got the job and the money.

I should add that acting should be a last resort. It's never worked for me (and in fact led to some pretty awkward moments with Phil Griffin). At some point in your life, you have got to know your value. It's your job to feel it and communicate it effectively. A strong sense of self-worth will serve you well in your relationship with your employer, and in any other relationship.

How Not to Ask

Many of us need to rethink the way we ask for promotions and raises, because when we do ask, it often ain't pretty. Just listen to the answers I hear when I ask, "Are there differences in the way men and women ask you for raises and promotions?"

> *I know you're busy, I know you don't*
> *have time . . .* —VALERIE JARRETT

Obama advisor Valerie Jarrett has been the boss in a variety of work-places. When I ask whether she sees a difference in approach between men and women asking for raises and promotions, she says, "Amazingly, men are almost detached from it emotionally. They're really comfortable. . . . Women are much more timid and appreciative and polite. Men are very matter-of-fact, businesslike, unemotional. It isn't really personal."

"Women are emotional?" I ask.

"Emotional in the sense of apologetic . . . I remember one woman in particular who started with, 'I know you're busy, I know you don't have time . . .'"

"Basically saying, 'Don't give me the raise'?"

"She backed into it badly, is the way I would say it," Valerie tells me.

"Apologetic" and "tentative" are two adjectives I heard over and over. Former editor-in-chief of *Newsweek,* cofounder of *The Daily Beast,* and founder of Tina Brown Live Media, Tina Brown says women often start to apologize with their body language before they even open their mouth. Then they'll begin by saying, "Well, you know, I've been here for a while and I've been thinking a lot about this . . . men come in and they just say, 'Hey, I'm not doing this anymore unless I get X.' And you think, 'Of course, of course, of course,' you know, you must take care of Joe, Fred, whomever. But women don't do that. They just come in and they look sad . . . and we can't do that!"

*I didn't really want to come to you
with this* . . . —CAROL BARTZ

I ask former Yahoo! CEO Carol Bartz, "Have you ever had a woman ask for a raise and apologize for imposing?"

"Oh, absolutely," she says. Bartz trots out a few she's heard: "'I didn't really want to come to you with this, but, gosh, do you think my bonus percentage could be higher?' And, 'Gee, could you just think about it?' When they say, 'I don't know if you'll consider . . . ,' right away they are giving you an out. Of course I wouldn't consider, you just told me not to consider . . . when somebody gives you the reason you can say no, it just makes your job easier."

And men?

Men will say, "'I believe I'm undervalued here,'" Bartz tells me. "And that's always code for 'I'm going someplace where they value me, and it's for these reasons.'"

"When men ask for raises there's always some cost," ad exec Donny Deutsch says. "It's always 'because I did this' and 'if I don't get the raise. . . .' There's always [an imaginary] gun to the head, some gamesmanship. First of all, women don't ask as much. And when they do ask, it's not 'Give it to me or else.'"

When you combine my experience with what I heard from the bosses above, I have to say, we women stink at this. Just look at our best opening lines:

- "I'm sorry."
- "I know you're busy."
- "I don't know if you have the time."
- "I don't know if you'll consider . . ."
- "I don't know if this is possible . . ."
- "I hate to do this."
- "I don't know if there's room for this in the budget."
- "I'm sorry if the timing is bad."

I think I've managed to use every one of those phrases in my attempts to get a raise. Of course, I used an additional strategy too—what former *More* editor Lesley Jane Seymour calls "playing the victim card." Seymour says women "present their personal challenges, saying things like, 'Well, I have this situation' or 'I have that burden' or 'My mother is ill and I have to support her' or whatever. Women present their cause, and you have to realize it's not a manager's job to support your causes, whatever they might be. . . . The companies can't say, 'Oh, I feel sorry for you.'"

How to Ask

Professor Hannah Riley Bowles has done research which supports the idea that playing the victim card is unlikely to work, because it's an explanation that's all about you; a more effective argument is one that taps into the organization's interests. You have to explain why a raise would make sense to the person you're talking with and to the company as a whole. She says the less effective route is "going in and laying down your credit card and saying, 'I can't buy the shoes I want to buy.'"

Bowles says the smarter approach is, for instance, if my request for a raise had been denied but I still wanted MSNBC to cover my hair/makeup/wardrobe costs, I might have said something like, "I think it makes sense for this job to have an expense account." I could have tried enlisting Phil's support in my efforts to project a professional image because my personal presentation has a direct impact on the show.

Bowles offers another tactic: "[One executive woman] told me she found out that a couple of subordinates of hers were being paid more than she was. She tried going in and basically referring to it as an error that she knew the company would want to correct. Obviously the company is not going to want subordinates paid more than superiors, right?" Bowles's latest research shows that women are more successful when they explain the appropriateness of their request in a way that communicates their desire to maintain good relationships at work. "The trick is trying to do both of these things at the same time and in a way that feels authentic and fits within the norms of the company," she says.

Suze Orman says the way to get what you want is to offer your boss a choice. "You should never, ever, ever ask a yes or no question. If you ask for a 10 percent raise and the boss says no, what are you going to say?" Instead, she suggests giving your boss two options: slightly more than what you want and then a lower number that you actually expect to get. "So you would say, 'I really think I deserve a 10 percent or 12 percent raise. Which one would you like to give me?' At that point the boss really doesn't know what to say, because that's not a yes or no question, and the power has shifted into your court. It's very difficult for anyone to come back and say 'Neither.'"

Vice president, publisher, and chief revenue officer for *Harper's Bazaar*, Carol Smith, tells me that the way men do it is to take the emotion out and simply say, "I've earned this. I'm coming in because here's what I've done over the last year, and now I've earned this raise." But she's always taken a softer approach: "I've often said that I don't want to be paid more, but I never want to be paid less. I want to be paid equal to the man sitting next to me who's bringing in the same amount of revenue."

Nora Ephron echoed those sentiments. "The words 'favored nations'—that's an expression all women should know," she says, underscoring the importance of knowing what the more highly compensated employees (the "favored nations") are making. "In other words, you always want to be paid no less than what anyone else is being paid. If you're at all a wussy about valuing yourself, you can't be a wussy about the words *favored nations*. All you're asking for is what everyone else is making."

Valerie Jarrett uses the same favored nations argument, but with a different delivery. "I don't like to negotiate salary at all, and one way I've compensated for that is by saying to someone, 'I expect that you'll be fair to me,' and then when they're not, I talk back. I say, 'I know you'll treat me fairly so you decide.' Then I come back and tell them they can do better."

Of course, saying "I expect you'll be fair to me" implies that both employer and employee share an understanding of what "fair" means. If you've done your homework, you know what both women and men with comparable experience and skill sets are making at your level.

Asking for More

Kate White urges women to push the envelope. "You cannot be afraid to ask for more. But you have to do it in a way that is not emotional. . . . What you really have to do is make it about what your value is," she says. "Stay very neutral and say, 'I'm very happy to have the offer. It sounds like a great job. I was looking for $90,000 based on my experience and skills.' They always—almost always—have more. As a boss I know that if you really want somebody, except in a recession where sometimes your hands are tied, you can go back and get more."

White says that after years of working in women's magazines and publishing articles about women's issues, she learned not to apologize and not to overexplain. But it takes practice. She says that when you try to negotiate an offer, management might very well be shocked by your audacity. In which case, "You've got to learn to be very careful and keep it neutral and light, like a game," White tells me. You have to walk a line between being too deferential and too aggressive, and you have to learn to recognize when the line has been crossed. But practice makes perfect.

"Every time you have one of those conversations, you get better at it. I had a situation once where I was using a lawyer, and they were giving the lawyer a terrible time. Basically they were indicating that they were getting frustrated with me because they felt I was asking for too much. I went in myself at that point and had a conversation, and in that conversation I realized, okay, I've got to back off a little. I said some things like, 'I sense I've really frustrated the hell out of you. I'm sorry about that.'"

Is White really recommending that women apologize for putting a number on their worth? "I wasn't apologizing for what I was asking. I was apologizing that the lawyer's situation had frustrated them," she explains. "I corrected the situation in fifteen minutes and I remember the lawyer later said to me, 'You're better at this than you're giving yourself credit for.' I think that the more you do, the more you step back and learn from the previous experiences. I try to pay attention to body language, and of course to whether I get what I want in the end, so that the next time I can take all of that into consideration."

Be Persistent

Stanford Professor Frank Flynn says that when women negotiate, they aren't as persistent as men are. "It's not that they don't ask, they don't ask ten times. And that's often the difference I see between women and men in business. Women assume no means no in a negotiation, and the negotiation is over." Flynn says men hear no as a signal "to take a different tack."

Suze Orman insists that if you're discussing a raise with your boss and you're not getting anywhere, "No matter how uncomfortable your boss tries to make you feel, I want you to stay right in your seat and keep the conversation going. If you know the company is on shaky financial ground, then of course you have to take that into consideration. But if the company is profitable and you are in fact a contributor to that profit, then you are not to walk out empty-handed." She suggests asking for another review in six months, and asking (and getting in writing) what raise to expect at that time. Meanwhile, ask for more vacation time or flexibility or whatever will be valuable to you. Orman says, "You must get something of value, for you are not on sale."

I can tell you from personal experience that all is not lost if you don't get what you deserve the first time around. Look at me: I had to go back a half dozen times! You may very well encounter resistance, even bullying, but there's much to be gained by holding your ground when you're presented with an offer that doesn't benefit you.

Women throw around the emotional thing.

—LESLEY JANE SEYMOUR

CoveyClub founder and former *More* editor Lesley Jane Seymour tells me a story about two female friends who got new jobs at the same company. They were negotiating with a senior woman at the firm. Seymour says, "When they got the job offer, they each said, 'Let me have my lawyer look at this,' and they were told 'Oh, that would mean starting out on the wrong foot, let's not go down that road . . . so why don't you just sign right here.'" Seymour says she was appalled when her friends—two "very savvy women"—ended up signing without having their deals reviewed by an attorney.

"When I found out these two friends of mine did that, I said to them, 'Do you mean to tell me that you signed this thing without a lawyer looking at it?' I said, 'Do you think the woman who did this to you would ever sign her contract without a lawyer looking at it?' And the answer is no. . . . To me that was something that only a woman would do to a woman. Women know women respond to that. No woman would say that to a man, because a man sitting across the table would say, 'This has nothing to do with starting out on the wrong foot, this is business . . . I'm taking it to my lawyer,' and that would have been the end of the discussion."

Writer, editor, and speaker Kate White has a similar story about being pressured when accepting an offer. Years ago she was being pursued by *Working Woman* magazine. She went to talk to the owner, but at the time she wasn't really looking for a job. But the owner made her an offer almost immediately. White was caught off-guard and wanted some time to think about making a move, but her prospective employer was giving her the full-court press. He wanted to make a fast hire, so he offered to sweeten the deal by giving her some equity in the company and kept calling her the next day.

She says she found herself dodging the owner's calls, still trying to weigh the offer's pros and cons. "Finally I called him back and said, 'Look, I don't think this is right for me,' but he really just pressured me. He was a fabulous sales guy on the phone. And I felt so guilty because I had stalled, and I couldn't really think of the right reason I couldn't go, so I buckled and said yes. . . . Later I wondered, 'How did I let myself get into this?' But I kept telling myself, 'at least I've got the equity.'"

Looking back, White says, she just wasn't sufficiently comfortable in her own skin to say, "I don't care if he's pressuring me; I need to do what's right for me. I should have said to him, 'Look, you caught me off-guard, offering me the job; I'm going to need a couple of days to really think this through.'"

If the Answer Is No

Valerie Jarrett says her best advice comes from the lesson her parents taught her, "which is a hard lesson to learn, and that's to not be afraid of rejection. It's okay. Men aren't afraid of rejection. They're taught both personally and professionally that it's a part of the game. It's why men ask women on dates; they ask ten women out and if one says yes, that's great. Women would have a very hard time with nine rejections out of ten. You wear it on your sleeve. My parents always said to me, 'If you don't try, you're certainly not going to get what you want, so it's okay to fail and learn from your failure.' You should have enough self-confidence to pick yourself back up and get back on your feet. You have to reach high. I think women are willing to settle for a much smaller promotion. What's wrong with asking for the bigger promotion? You think people will think less of you if you do, but they actually think more of you."

Carol Smith was the first female ad salesperson for the *Wall Street Journal* at a time when women weren't doing that job. She says she must have some male gene in her makeup because she's "always been a very strong negotiator when it comes to salaries." But she knows plenty of brilliant women who have a hard time being paid their value and who have an equally tough time with rejection.

She burst into tears ... a hugely successful woman.
—CAROL SMITH

Smith knows that emotions can handicap women at any age, and at any point in their career. She shares a story of a friend of hers who had recently taken on a great deal of additional work: "She had been doing basically three jobs in the last six months and had asked to be compensated. I knew what that job was worth because I'd had that job. So she was out to lunch with her boss and asked for the raise, and he said no. And she burst into tears." Smith points out that her friend wasn't a young woman, but an experienced executive. "I have known her for twenty years. She is brilliant, a hugely successful woman.

"She felt embarrassed and beaten down by this . . . she was going to walk away in tears, you know, and never go back." Smith told her friend that her boss's "no" didn't have to be the end. Smith encouraged her to go back and work out a solution that both she and her employer could accept.

Smith tells me, "It helped me that I came out of sales. When you're in sales you have to learn to get rejected and constantly go back. When most of my non-sales female colleagues hear 'no,' they take it personally, and they think, 'Oh, I must not deserve this.' . . . When you're in sales, you've got to ask for that order over and over and over again, and you have to figure out a way to go ask for it a different way and say the same thing with a different ending."

Be Ready to Walk

Sometimes when the answer is no, you realize you're not going to get what you want now, or possibly ever. That's when you realize it's time to get out. Tina Brown remembers the moment she realized it was time to leave Condé Nast. "I was editor at the *New Yorker*, my contract was coming up, and I wanted to play more of a role in the strategy of the magazine instead of just the editing. And the president of the company, Steve Florio, took me to lunch. I started to talk about how this was an issue in my contract. And he said to me, 'Where are you going to go? No one's going to give you a dress allowance like we do.'" Those words had her packing her bags.

Carol Bartz suggests that when push comes to shove, you better have your bags packed: "Now, what I will say to you is, you have to be ready to walk . . . I mean, when you are in a situation and you take a stand, you've got to be ready for the consequences. You know, when they look you in the eye and realize, 'This crazy bitch is going to leave.'"

If you deserve a raise, simply say it. But be prepared to leave and work somewhere else if management doesn't agree.

Former GE CEO Jack Welch says that successful salary negotiations depend on your level of confidence; if you know your skills are valuable, you know you'll find another, better job. "If you think it's easy for a guy to go in there and ask for money, I'm not sure it is. . . . I always felt if I didn't get what I liked, I was packing it in," he says. "I was ready to leave the day before I became chairman. I was always ready to pack it in, because I thought I could do well elsewhere."

Writer Nora Ephron told me that quitting can be the best thing for your career: "You have to look at what men do. They quit, and they go somewhere else." That's how they improve their salaries quickly. But unless you like being unemployed, you need to be talking to other companies all the time and have an idea of where you're headed next. "The way to do it is you say, 'I need more money, I'm not being paid as much as so and so,' and you have to be prepared to leave. But you have to go sneak around and find somewhere to go. That's a very important thing, having somewhere to go when you quit," she said.

Comedian and talk show host Joy Behar will always have somewhere to go when she quits. She maintains her independence by keeping her comedy skills sharp. "One of the things that I've done in my career over the years is to have many irons in the fire," Behar tells me.

"When I took *The View*, I did a lot of stand-up because nobody in television was going to control me. I could always make a living on the road." Now she has both *The View* and her own show, but she still does stand-up just to keep her options open.

Suze Orman points out that you can take the strongest negotiating stance of all when you have your financial safety net in place. "A woman can only be powerful when she doesn't need the money, otherwise she can't be powerful. You can't push somebody and say, 'This is what I want.' If you really need it and they let you go, what are you going to do?"

But Suze, how many women who ask for raises don't actually need the money? Orman responds, "What I'm saying is, the time to go in and ask for a raise with confidence is not when you have credit card debt, it's when you have an eight-month emergency fund. You also have to have a plan. Know your alternatives and come from a powerful place, not an insecure place. What gives you power? The answer is usually 'having money to fall back on.' You don't have to have a lot, just enough for you to know you'll be okay no matter what."

Orman recommends taking into account your entire financial picture before you start talking to your boss about money: "Not just what you're earning, but where is your money invested? How is it invested? Do you have all your wills and trusts? Do you have your insurance in place? Is everything together that creates a powerful woman? Because if it's not, you're walking into a negotiation powerless, and you will never be able to get the amount of money that you deserve because you're coming from a powerless place. It really is as simple as that."

She's right: The fact that I was in the red at the end of every month probably gave me an air of desperation. What I needed was an air of confidence.

When I tell Donny Deutsch that I had been an idiot about negotiating, he responds, "Well, then next time you're ready to do it, you talk to me first." The idea that Deutsch might be a more effective advocate for me than I am for myself speaks volumes about how powerless I was to get the money I deserved. And I think if most women really would look in the mirror, they'd see they aren't nearly as powerful as they should be either.

CHAPTER 7

ALLIES AND ENEMIES

A New Appreciation of Men in the Workplace, and a Warning About Women

My story, with Sheila Bair, Hannah Riley Bowles, Marie C. Wilson, Susie Essman, Tina Brown, Arianna Huffington, Victoria Budson, and Brooksley Born

About to Walk

When I got back to New York after the 2008 presidential primary season, I was demoralized and exhausted. After some soul-searching, I realized I could not go on being undervalued. I could not allow any managers, male or female, to exploit my insecurities. I could not back down anymore. After years of letting myself be pushed around in an unforgiving profession, I was finally mature enough to know that when it came to being rewarded for my value, I was my own worst enemy.

Now was the time to make it right.

That is what brought me to the meeting with Joe at the Rock Center Café. I felt Joe deserved an explanation. He had, after all, believed in me when no one else did. He had revitalized my career, and now I had to walk away.

I was transparent with Joe about the mistakes I had made. I also made it clear that whatever my own failings in getting my worth, the current pay structure between us was wrong. I had allowed it to persist for too long. I felt nauseated when I told him I would be leaving this job and a show that we both fought so hard to create.

"I've been working on something," he said. "Please wait another week. I have an idea. I see this as my business, and I see you as important to the success of that business. I need a chance to find a way to make you stay and feel whole. I won't ask for too much time. Just a few days."

A week later I went online to my checking account thinking I had run through my funds. I was expecting once again to be overdrawn and at least $2,000 in the red. Instead, I was shocked to find that I had more money in my bank account than I ever had had in my life.

I had not received the raise that I was looking for and was still not being paid what I deserved, but NBC had direct deposited a large amount of money into my account. Questions started racing through my mind.

Where did this money come from? (Had I won the lottery?) Would NBC give me a huge bonus without telling me first? (Not on your life.) Did the crack GE accountants accidentally add a few extra zeros to my paycheck? (A remote possibility.)

I soon learned, to my horror, that Joe had demanded that MSNBC transfer his ratings bonuses to my account. These were payments Joe had negotiated in his contract. They were bonuses he received if *Morning Joe* ratings topped that of the Imus show, which we had replaced. While management never expected we could do that so quickly, Joe had banked on our success and soon tripled his salary.

So the money NBC had added to my account was actually subtracted from Joe's compensation.

I was furious. Raging. Humiliated. How could I accept this money? How weak and dependent would this make me look? How could NBC allow this?

Joe and I had ridiculous, loud arguments over whether I could accept his bonus pay. While it is interesting to look at the situation now that Joe and I are together, at this time we were years away from being anything more than colleagues and friends. Joe's decision to do this had nothing to do with any personal relationship with me but was based entirely upon the value I brought to the show and to him. He wanted his good salary to continue. He was smart to know the show was nothing without me. But why didn't I know that?

Although his public persona is quite different, when it comes to negotiations, Joe is introspective and calculating. Sensing that he was about to lose the cohost who would help him earn even more money down the line, Joe had thought through his options for keeping me on *Morning Joe*. Soon he realized there was only one course of action. Joe would sign over parts of his ratings bonuses or lose his cohost, and possibly the success of *Morning Joe*.

To Joe's agent and NBC, it seemed like a supremely generous gift to a cohost. To Joe, it had less to do with charity than it did with the bottom line: I was a good investment.

While I understood the argument intellectually, I was still not emotionally prepared to accept a handout from a professional partner whom I considered to be my equal. So I did what I often did when confronted with a professional or personal crisis: I called my dad.

After I spent way too long explaining the situation, my father was ready to render a speedy verdict.

"Mika, it sounds like a shrewd business strategy on Joe's part. He is worth much more with you as his partner on the show than he is by himself. CEOs reward top performers with bonuses all the time. What makes this any different?"

That was a good question, and I had no good answer. My father was right. I would take the bonuses, not because I needed them but because I deserved them.

Joe's move had been generous, but as both my father and Joe pointed out, it was also a shrewd business move. We had a show that was on the upswing, whether MSNBC management could see it or not. He didn't want me to leave, he knew I was important to the show, and he knew that what was happening within the walls of 30 Rock was not right. He actually said that to the management: "You can be part of a *New York Times* article about our salary discrepancy, but I'm not." As is his habit, Joe Scarborough once again took matters into his own hands.

My frustration with my employer did not subside. I was emboldened by the fact that I knew I deserved the money. The investment that Joe had made—and that's what it was, not a donation but an investment—made me realize something about myself that apparently I hadn't known, even then. And that is, I was worth more. I mean absolutely, positively, unequivocally worth more. Why should I let Joe make up for MSNBC's shortfall? That was not going to continue; I was done. I finally knew my value and could not stay unless my employer recognized it, too. This problem was MSNBC's creation, but it was up to me to fix it.

I walked back into Phil's office, sat down, and spoke. My voice was low and sounded different, but it was me talking. Really talking. Not acting. Not venting. Not whining. Just talking in my own words: "You are a bad boyfriend. Do you know what that is, Phil?"

I didn't wait for a response.

"You take and take and take, but never give. Start giving," I said.

I went into great detail on the definition of a "bad boyfriend." It was a little weird, and I probably wasn't saying just the right things, but it was calm and completely from the heart. Even better, I was ready to walk out the door with nothing and leave MSNBC for good. And the company knew it.

Phil actually took a moment, and then said, "You're right. We will fix this. I will fix this."

Time had also passed since our talk, and we had had a chance to get to know each other.

Within months, I had a new contract. It wasn't perfect. I am still paid considerably less than Joe, but at least I'm moving in the right direction. I got a good deal at a tough economic time for the network. They came through, but more importantly, I came through for myself. What Joe did, his conviction and follow-through, emboldened me. He gave me the confidence and drive to make MSNBC compensate me directly. The bottom line was, this time I really *was* ready to walk. You get paid your value when you're ready to walk. And by the way, if you're worth nothing, you'll be walking anyway. So you have to know your worth, then be ready to walk out the door.

The Value of Strategic Alliances

Still, I could not get over the fact that it took a man to turn the tide. I was angry, mostly at myself, that it had to come to that. A man giving a woman money in the workplace just didn't feel right to me. Joe set me straight: "You are taking yourself way too seriously. This isn't about you. This is about me making more money. Because if you stay, our ratings will go up. And that will mean more money for my family. Stop thinking that I am being generous to you. This is really a selfish business decision about me."

I have cut a number of business deals for others and myself since that famous "bad boyfriend" talk with Phil. I have stepped in as an agent and dealmaker for several of NBC's female stars. I pay it forward every chance that I get. I am now at a point where negotiation is fun for me—especially when I am helping another woman discover her value.

But back then, as Joe fought to keep me on *Morning Joe*, he pored over my contract and salary and then guaranteed me that between TV, radio, and books, I would equal the salary I earned at CBS News. I was skeptical, but he laughed me off.

"You don't know your value!" he would say. "You will be laughing all the way to the bank."

By the end of the year, he had made good on all his guarantees and more. I got a book deal, a radio show, and other business opportunities. Looking back, it occurred to me that Joe knew my value even better than I did, and he became offended and aggressive when others did not.

This experience has taught me the importance of having allies. Why not accept help from people who value you? Men do it all the time. And by allies, I don't mean agents. Agents were helpless to get me the money I deserved. The fact is, no one—no one—can negotiate for you. I may use an agent to handle paperwork and money and details and mechanics, absolutely. But when it comes to speaking for me, I have to do that.

Several women I interviewed mentioned having mentors who offered valuable assistance in their careers. Sheila Bair speaks both of mentors and of other influential men who helped clear a path for her.

Throughout my career,
I've been mentored by men. —SHEILA BAIR

For seven years, Bair worked as counsel to Senate Majority Leader Robert Dole and credits him with paving the way for her. "He was a big supporter of women, and he had a lot of senior women on the staff," Bair says. "Women with real power, not just symbols; they were true advisors to him. Especially back when I was starting my career, there weren't that many women to mentor you, because there just weren't that many [to begin with]. Sandra Day O'Connor, Elizabeth Dole. I can count prominent women on my fingers and toes, so we did rely on men . . . Throughout my career, I've been mentored by men."

Bair tells me that during the financial crisis, it was Federal Reserve Chairman Ben Bernanke who helped her get her message across: "He was the one who first started really listening, especially on some of the bailout issues. . . . Of course, that helped because Ben had a lot of credibility with the guys."

But what Joe had done for me was more than endorse my ideas. I had started thinking of him as a business partner, someone whose help I could accept without giving up control. But he'd done more than even an ordinary business partner. He had actually used his own paycheck, in addition to his personal influence, to advance my interests.

People who study gender and negotiation would call him a sponsor: someone who is willing to use their own social capital to help pull another up the corporate ladder.

Harvard's Hannah Riley Bowles says, "We do need men to sponsor women very badly; they're in positions of power. When men in a position of power decide to clear that path for you—make sure you get the right exposure, make sure you get to the right meetings—that means a great deal. And there are not that many women to do that for you, frankly. A lot of the women at the top reach back, but there's just not enough of them."

Sponsorship is more than mentorship. A mentor will advise an employee, give him or her feedback, offer career strategy, and explain the company culture. Companies invest considerable resources in mentoring programs, but research shows that mentoring doesn't necessarily translate into better jobs for women. Women can be mentored so much that it wastes their time. Sponsors, on the other hand, will do more by using their connections and their influence to advocate for an employee.

Sponsorship is someone who advocates for you when you are not in the room. —VICTORIA BUDSON

Victoria Budson, founding Executive Director of the Women and Public Policy Program at Harvard University, explains further, "There is a lot of talk about mentorship, and when you meet with women across all sectors, they will often talk about the need for a mentor. Now, a mentor is someone who, when you are in the room with them, you ask their advice or reach out to them directly. And they share their knowledge to help you find your career path, to help you navigate organizations or situations; very helpful.

"However, sponsorship is also important. Sponsorship is someone who advocates for you when you are not in the room. And having a sponsor do that enables you to be put up for opportunities that you might not even know about. And if your sponsor is in a different social network than you, it can also give you credibility and access through that sponsor to discussions, opportunities, and outcomes that you would not have had access to otherwise."

Catalyst's research finds that "high-potential women are over-mentored and undersponsored relative to their male peers—and that they are not advancing in their organizations." Without sponsorship, women are not only less likely than men to move up, but they're also more hesitant to pursue top roles.

Lack of sponsorship, mentors, and networks: this was a recurring theme in almost all my conversations on the subject of women and compensation. Women's advocate Marie C. Wilson says women just don't have the same useful connections that men do, and the effects can be profound: "In the finance industry and some of the more masculine legal industries, women are not part of those networks that men are a

part of, whether it's golf or the clubs that they take people to at night.
. . . And who gets seen, who gets promoted, are people who are a part
of those networks." She also says that we have to find ways to make
men more comfortable with sponsoring the opposite sex. "If you are a
man, taking on a young man as a sponsor is much easier than taking
on a young woman because there is a certain kind of tension about that
relationship; people look at it differently."

Like me, many of the highly successful women I interviewed had
also received significant help from men in their industry. Susie Essman
tells the story of trying to join the Friars Club, a century-old private
club for entertainment-industry types, notably comedians, that's really
a tale about sponsorship. Traditionally all-male, the Friars Club didn't
allow women members until 1988, and women weren't invited to their
famed Celebrity Roasts. Essman says, "When they first asked me to do
roasts, they didn't allow women to even sit on the dais . . . [the men's
jokes] were all filthy, dirty, blue blue blue, and they didn't think our
delicate ears could handle it. So when I first had to do a roast, I had
to prove that I could be as dirty as them and yet not be vulgar. I had
to keep that balance." Naturally, Essman proved herself, managing to
be both feminine and filthy dirty, and also stay on point and deliver a
punch line.

Years later, "there was a roast that Comedy Central was recording
for Jerry Stiller," Essman says. "The Friars Club had put my name in
because I had proven myself with all these old guys—Alan King and
all these great old comics—who did not think women were funny
at all. Comedy Central turned me down. They didn't want me on,
and I do believe it was because I was a woman of a certain age and
they wanted guys that were in their early twenties. The Friars Club,
to their credit, fought for me to be on because I had proven myself
over and over again. They put me on the show and I killed, and Larry
David saw me on that show and called me up and gave me the part
in *Curb*."

As Essman points out, "In show business, it takes one person to say, 'You know what, you're really good.'" It took Larry David, creator of HBO's *Curb Your Enthusiasm*, "who was a very powerful person in the comedy world, to say, 'I think this person is really talented and I'm going to give her a part on my show.'"

When I ask Essman whether she thinks a woman would have been able to do the same for her, she tells me, "I do think there are women in the business who would have been able to do that for me; there have been powerful women in the business. I don't think there are many. People say comedy is a man's world, but the world is a man's world."

Clearly, the more people you know—the more people who are willing to support your efforts—the more likely you are to succeed, and the more likely you are to be paid well. Research has shown that success really does depend on who you know. A study published in *Administrative Science Quarterly* looked at the effects of different personal attributes on compensation and found that in terms of salary, candidates who knew just one person in the organization negotiated salaries that were 4.7 percent higher than those without social ties.

Professor Hannah Riley Bowles points out, "In general, we could certainly say, the better you know people, the more information they're likely to share, the more helpful they're likely to be to you. They can vouch for you, they can help you negotiate, they can lend social capital. They can say, 'This person is really . . . ,' they can present you in a very favorable light. There are a variety of things they can do in terms of quality of information that you get, the way you present yourself, knowing whom to talk to, knowing how to present yourself. You have to be authentic to yourself, but you also have to negotiate the way that fits the norms of the organization."

Harvard's Victoria Budson also recommends stepping outside of your perceived network. She explains, "I think it is important to remember, though you may learn valuable tools and lessons from someone who is like you, however you define that, [someone unlike you can be even more valuable]. Maybe your mentor is an engineer like you, an African-American woman like you, someone who went to college or university like you, but that gives you access to a network where you already have some information or data. You may want to look for a sponsor or mentor also who is in a very different circle and network. Both can be very constructive."

But Victoria knows that asking for this kind of support in the workplace can be difficult. She suggests targeting the type of mentor or sponsor you want, and then putting yourself in the right context so that asking that person for support feels natural, and mutually beneficial. So what steps should someone take? "A part of it is really putting yourself in different situations where you will have, if you can, work interactions and work performances that this person will see. Sometimes, it means you just reach out to them in the organization—you have to always be mindful of what your organizational culture is. Will it be productive for you to build the relationship? You are someone in a different unit; will it be productive for you to build the relationship with someone at a different level and how do you manage and navigate that within your organization?" Asking yourself these questions and putting yourself in these situations can help lead to an effective sponsorship relationship.

Tina Brown, founder of Tina Brown Live Media, notes a difference in the quality of men's networks and women's networks. She points out that women just don't have the long history in the workplace that amounts to a female networking tradition. "I think that a networking background for women is just not there. When men get fired from these jobs, these big jobs, they have other men who step forward to look after them and get them jobs as presidents of this, or think tanks, or some big nonprofit. I mean, you see men being taken care of when they're fired. When I see women getting fired, there's no cushion of networking waiting to deploy them into other jobs. I just don't see it. I see men all the time being fired from their jobs and being looked after by their networks. . . . Women just don't have the deep bench of network."

But as I listen to women's stories and tell my own, I wonder whether part of the reason that women's networks aren't as powerful is because women aren't trying very hard to support one another.

Sisterhood Is Powerful . . . Isn't It?

Many of my interviewees cite evidence that other women not only weren't there to lend a hand, but they were actively undermining their efforts to get ahead.

Are women harder on other women? It may just be that women managers are more effective with women because they know which buttons to push. Who better to exploit the weaknesses that hold women back than a woman? I'm reminded of Lesley Jane Seymour's story about the female manager who discouraged Seymour's friends from having their contracts reviewed by a lawyer.

Women need to learn how to respond to these tactics.

> *I see all women advancing in the workplace the second the women change their perspective on women.* —LIZ BENTLEY

Executive coach Liz Bentley is the founder of Liz Bentley Associates, a consulting firm specializing in leadership development programs for both individuals and companies. She is also the person I trust to coach contestants at my national Know Your Value events. And when we sat down to speak for this book, Liz emphasized the importance of women standing up for each other.

She tells me, "We can talk all day long about telling women to advocate for themselves, have a strong voice, be more confident, lean in, and do this also in your personal life. But if as women, every time we see women doing that, we're sabotaging them, stabbing them in the back, talking poorly about them, then it will never work. All of this is just a waste of time."

Liz knows, from her experiences coaching both men and women, how often women are their own biggest adversaries and she encourages women to pay attention to their own behaviors. "When a woman is strong and advocates for herself and does all the things the guys do, how quickly do (other women) rally around her and say, 'Hey, that's fantastic'?"

When I asked for an example of this phenomenon from one of her clients, she describes, "I was talking to someone about real estate and they would say things like [in a dismissive, snarky tone], 'Well, you know, she's a broker and she gets all of her clients from just, like, the tennis club.'"

She continues, "Now, let me say it again in a male's voice. 'Ahh, he's a great golfer and he's amazing and he gets so many of his leads from his golf game.' Two different voices, right? So that's the kind of thing women do to each other all day long.

"So instead of saying, 'That's so awesome. That's really super great. She's killing it!' we're resentful she got so many great connections from the tennis club. We look at the men and reward them for doing things, and when women do it, we criticize them. That's the biggest mistake, in my opinion. And if we change that, all women advance in the workplace.

"I see all women advancing in the workplace the second the women change their perspective on women."

What follows is an example of what I've done, and it is a textbook case of what not to do. I repeat: Women managers know all too well what strategies to use to keep us cheap.

The Middle Manager, a Woman,
Tells Me Not to Get That Raise

Ironically, the only time I was brought to tears at MSNBC over my pay problems was in a conversation with a middle manager who happened to be a woman.

She called a meeting to discuss my salary dispute, and the mood quickly turned sour. This manager insisted that I back off my request for a pay raise and told me that my demands were badly timed. Then she really dug in: "Mika, people won't like you. You are going to get a bad reputation. You need to stop." This woman knew Joe's salary was fourteen times mine—a huge disparity. But she was skilled at getting me to change my focus.

She kept me in her office for thirty minutes, arguing that I would ruin my reputation and that my request for more equitable pay would cost me in popularity. She said this with a clear warning in her voice, even a threat. "People will see you as a problem," she said. She told me I should be focused less on earning my value and more on winning MSNBC's Miss Congeniality prize. Was she serious? Sadly, she was—and her strategy worked.

Looking back on that day years later, I cannot believe how naïve I was. I was shocked to tears that a woman would push another woman to accept such a degrading situation. I am even more pained to admit that I actually started worrying about whether my coworkers would stop liking me if I pressed for the raise that I so clearly deserved. It was obvious to this female manager that while I was used to being liked in newsrooms, I had no idea what it was like to be paid a salary that matched my worth. So she did what any effective manager would do: She went in for the kill.

When it comes to gender politics, how women treat other women in the workplace is a sensitive and fraught topic. I've had wonderful female bosses and not-so-wonderful ones. I've spoken with women who loved their female bosses and those who described relationships with female bosses that were complicated by generational experience and by differences in life choices. And several times since *Morning Joe* began, a female manager played into my feminine fears and tendencies with the sole intent of holding me back. The Paris Hilton incident, the red hair clip reprimand, this dressing-down when I asked for a raise: The most painful and least constructive confrontations I've had in my career have been with women. Ladies, we should be ashamed of ourselves. In the highest levels of business, we are our own worst enemies. Before we can fix this problem, we first have to admit to it.

Arianna Huffington believes it's vitally important for women to be truly supportive of one another: "Indeed, I talk about building our 'fearlessness tribe,' surrounding ourselves with women—and men, of course!—who will always be in our corner, always there for us, whether we succeed or fail.

"It's very important for older women, those who have gone before, to give a hand up and to mentor younger women in a consistent, sustained way—which is ultimately sponsoring them. Finding a sponsor is very similar to asking for a raise: If you don't ask for help, no one is going to just give it to you.

"I think women need to do what men have always done: reach out and connect. In some ways, social media has made this easier. And there are more and more conferences for women, places to meet and learn from women who have done the things you are interested in doing." Huffington recently cohosted the WIE (Women: Inspiration & Enterprise) Symposium, with Sarah Brown and Donna Karan, bringing together women from all walks of life for inspiration and empowerment, and to take action for the betterment of all women.

I ask former CFTC chair Brooksley Born about the impediments women still face, and how she thinks we could overcome them. She, too, argues that women should be helping one another out. "It's really important for women to try to work together to change things in the workplace, to open opportunities, and I think it needs to be talked about. I think women need to support each other and cooperate with one another. They need to seek out male allies in the workplace, and they need to work as a group to change workplace policies to make them more amenable for women to be treated equally."

I ask her, "Do you think that women aren't helping other women? Or not helping them as much as they should?"

"Well, I think there's a need for more. I do think there's a lot of mutual support—not universal, obviously. But when there was a lot of discrimination, in the 1970s for example, it was easier to get people activated. Women consciously got together to network and work together and support each other in many big cities around the country. And I don't know the extent to which that is going on with the younger age groups today. Luckily there are a lot more venues where they can do it. There are wonderful Women's Bar Associations, and associations of women journalists, and associations that aren't gender-specific, for people who are like-minded to get together and work on these issues."

Born's last piece of advice for women coming up in the ranks today is exactly that—stick together and help each other. She encourages younger women "to make sure they are continuing to work together for more equal treatment and economic opportunities."

CHAPTER 8

MOTHERHOOD
The Game Changer

My story, with Sheila Bair, Senator Claire McCaskill, Lesley Jane Seymour,
Sheryl Sandberg, Norah O'Donnell, Carol Smith, Brooksley Born, Valerie Jarrett,
Tina Brown, Carol Bartz, Kate White, Victoria Budson, and Marie C. Wilson

Iowa and Beyond

Throughout my weeks on the road covering the primaries in 2008, I was scared to mention my two girls. A woman talking about her family seemed out of place at work. Joe freely talked to his children on the phone and talked about flying them to our various locations as we traveled state to state. But I never felt that I could. I suspected that the men I worked for might think less of me if I did. This was in my mind, not theirs.

I would call my family and tell them how much I missed them, and at times I deeply yearned for their presence. But you never saw it on my face when I was working. After all those years in the business, I still didn't feel comfortable "raising issues" about needing to be with my family. I suffered alone, as did they. I wish I had felt more comfortable, and I wish I could have afforded to bring them along and expose them to the story. Joe's ability to do that made me envious.

When it comes to wages and advancement, the gender gap is widest for working mothers.

Research shows that women's earnings go down for each child they have. Part of the gap in wages and advancement for mothers is because they take time out of the workforce or cut back on hours. But studies also indicate that even if they don't cut back, mothers still earn less.

Harvard's Victoria Budson offers more insight on how and why the gap persists. "There is very important research that shares with us that when women and men—who are equally competent within those studies—are compared, women with children fare worse than others. What we see is in nearly all industrialized nations; women do worse in the labor market. When they have children, they do worse than either men or women without kids."

This is a finding that has been repeatedly documented within the research community. And that leads us to question why; what's interesting is women are perceived, when they are mothers, as less competent and committed to their jobs. And so even when the actions show that women are unequivocally committed to and competent in their roles, they still get discriminated against. At work, competence and likeability in women is often seen as a seesaw (i.e., when competence goes up, women are perceived as less warm and less likeable).

Now, we all know that it isn't true. Women can be both warm and competent. However, the perception remains and the consequences are particularly impactful for mothers.

So if you're a competent mother—which presumably all mothers aspire to be—your upward climb is particularly steep. And the necessity of knowing your value, and vigilantly protecting it, increases.

In a study titled "Getting a Job: Is There a Motherhood Penalty?" researchers Shelley Correll, Stephen Benard, and In Paik of Cornell University asked participants to evaluate resumes for two equally qualified job candidates: one was a mother, the other was not. Mothers were consistently ranked as less competent and less committed than non-moms. They were also offered, on average, $11,000 a year less pay.

Representative Carolyn B. Maloney (D-NY), who is also the chairwoman of the Joint Economic Committee, recently commissioned a report based on an analysis of census data. "When working women have kids, they know it will change their lives, but they are stunned at how much it changes their paycheck," Maloney said. The data shows that across the workforce, the pay gap is slightly wider for managers who have children. Managers who are mothers typically earn seventy-nine cents of every dollar paid to managers who are fathers, and that gap has stayed the same for at least a decade. Could the difference be explained by discrimination?

Victoria Budson adds, "Women get a lot of social backlash. If they are warm and really nice, then we see them as less competent. And if women are really competent, then we see them as less warm, and we don't like them like that. Likeability has a real impact on how well you do within an organization."

Likeability has a real impact on how well you do within an organization. —VICTORIA BUDSON

Most mothers I spoke to were well-aware of the way they are perceived. Sheila Bair is the mother of two children. "Talking about family can be viewed negatively by men, like you're more focused on that than your work. Or that those are soft issues and you're not serious," she tells me. "I always come to work with a purpose, but I do think I generally do not talk a lot about my family in front of my male colleagues unless they initiate it. But some men love talking about their kids."

"Men look great when they're talking about their families," I say.

Bair agrees. "That's right, but women can be perceived as being diverted from our careers if we talk about our families."

I watched one focus group on me, and one woman called me Cruella de Vil. —CLAIRE MCCASKILL

Senator Claire McCaskill's (D-MO) career illustrates the mine-laden path to success that women must follow. McCaskill has spent the past three decades running for political office. Her first bid was for the job of Kansas City prosecutor, which she describes as "a very male-dominated world." At the time, McCaskill had just given birth. "I had just had my third child," she says, "and all my children were very young, and the traditional thing is to show your children to humanize you and so forth. When I ran for prosecutor, there was never a mention of my children, and I did that because I worried first that people would think, 'She has young children, she shouldn't have that job' . . . I was worried that people would think I wasn't tough enough to do the job, that I somehow wouldn't be able to come down hard on violent criminals.

"There had never been a woman elected to that office, and so I was trying to convince people. My commercials were all about the fact that the police had endorsed me and never mentioned the fact that I had three small children." McCaskill won the election.

Years later, McCaskill ran for governor, but she was defeated. During the campaign, her emphasis was to show people "that I was smart and that I was confident, that I could do this job." After McCaskill lost, a journalist told her, "[she] couldn't decide whether I was more the model of the obnoxious teacher's pet or the really obnoxious contestant on *Jeopardy!*. I had all the answers, but the feedback we seemed to get from the voters was that 'tough' was not the problem, competence was no longer a problem, it was whether or not they wanted to spend any time with me. You know—whether there was that likeability. It was just incredibly shocking to me that after spending my entire career worrying about showing everyone that I was up to the job . . . now all of a sudden I had to make sure they knew that I truly like to cook and I truly adore and worship my children."

Fast-forward a few more years. McCaskill ran for the Senate, and she once again struggled for that balance, making midcourse corrections. "When I was running, I watched one focus group on me, and one woman called me Cruella de Vil.

"So that's when I realized people need to understand that I've got a family, and I've got the same fears and hopes and dreams for my kids that they have. And so at that point in the Senate campaign, my daughter was in one of the commercials—my daughter and my mom.

"How do you walk the line between the b-word and ambition? It's a very narrow tightrope at times, and how you walk that tightrope is a challenge in and of itself," McCaskill tells me.

Lesley Jane Seymour, formerly of *More* magazine and now the founder of CoveyClub, an online-offline experience that connects women around the world, agrees that some women don't pull their equal weight at work. "There are people who can't do both," she says. "I've seen that on staff, people who just can't manage to do both, and you know, they're never here, they're out, or they're making excuses."

Seymour believes those examples reinforce the stereotype. "[Employers] have one bad employee who falls apart when they are trying to handle a family, so they assume no one can do it. And they don't know about all the other incredible women who you don't even know have children, because they manage it so well."

Facebook COO Sheryl Sandberg says she sees women struggling to balance family and work even before they have children. "It's very hard to watch," she tells me. "I've hired all these men and women, and then eight years later the men are largely ahead of the women. And the women were just as talented." She notices that it isn't necessarily that women aren't raising their hands and asking for promotions or new opportunities in general; it's that they're not pushing forward specifically during their child-bearing years.

The pattern is the following: A woman starts thinking about having a kid. Now maybe she's just thinking about it right as she gets engaged, maybe she starts thinking about it right as they start trying, but even if they're trying to get pregnant that minute, it's nine months to have the baby, three months of maternity leave, three months to catch your breath: That's already a year and a half. More likely they start thinking about this a year and a half before that, even two or three years, and at the moment they start making room for a kid, they stop looking for new opportunities. "They think, 'Oh my god, I want to have a child, there's no way I can fit anything more.' So the men around them are busy—solving problems, looking for new opportunities, saying, 'I want the promotion, I want the transfer, I want the raise, I want the new job'—and the women start leaning backward." Sandberg argues that by the time women turn their full attention back to work, they've been passed over.

"So what's the solution?" I ask. "Don't have kids?"

Sandberg replies, "Keep your foot on the gas. My advice is, when you have a child, you'll want to slow down, but don't slow down *in advance* of the child."

There's so much anecdotal evidence that having children impairs your ability to do well at work, but I sincerely believe that having children has made me a more valuable employee. The fact is, women like me overcompensate at work, to prove that having kids does not make us less effective. But we demand less in return for being so lucky to have kids and a job, as if someone gave us a gift when they doubled our workload and made sleep a thing of the past. This is something I have done throughout my career. I think the problem is that women buy into the idea that they can't contribute significantly both at work and at home, and as a consequence, they undervalue themselves.

It's a common problem that mothers underestimate their worth and their value. —NORAH O'DONNELL

Coanchor of *CBS This Morning* Norah O'Donnell, a colleague and a good friend, tells me, "I guess the truly honest answer is that I probably would ask for more if I did not have kids, and that's a tough thing to say. . . . I'm worried that I'll look like an ungrateful employee, that I'll seem ungrateful for the great job that I have.

"I think that it's a common problem that mothers underestimate their worth and their value. Mothers ask for less, demand less from their employers, because they already think that they are struggling with this balance of work and family . . . that guilt can then inhibit them from asking for more, because any free moment that they may have at work gives them an opportunity to make a doctor's appointment or a dentist's appointment or to order diapers online—but that is a false sense of guilt.

"I know that I'm there at work just as much as others; I work just as many long hours," O'Donnell continues. "I'm there before most people stroll into work, and I stay later. Mothers work hard and sometimes doubly hard, and are even more productive in some ways because they know they have only so much time to do that."

The truth is, in many cases, having children adds to our value. We may not be more organized, but we use time far more wisely. We have babies to protect, so our decision-making skills revolve around real-life issues. We develop another dimension to our lives that makes O'Donnell and me better reporters and storytellers. But with that also comes guilt. And it cuts both ways. We feel guilty that we can't give our kids more time—that goes without saying—but I believe working mothers also feel guilty about having great jobs. We feel that we're so blessed to have it all, and that feeling of luck undermines our ability to negotiate effectively, and gives managers the sense that we can be taken advantage of. We tend to work harder to prove that our kids won't be an impediment to our productivity. Take what the amazingly honest Carol Smith told me, which says it all:

I love hiring women [for] four days a week because they actually will produce at least five days' worth of work for four days' worth of pay. —CAROL SMITH

Former *Elle* publisher Carol Smith sees mothers undercutting their value. "I will say, as a person who has hired a lot of women who want to continue to work but also have their family, this whole idea of job shares and part time . . . they will do anything to have a four-day week. Anything. They will work in the bathroom. They will work twenty-four hours during the four days they work to be able to get that fifth day at home.

"The women who are striving to work part-time, whether it's three or four days a week, will sacrifice everything. And let's start with money. So if they're working four days a week, they don't say, 'I now want 80 percent.' They will accept 60 percent of their salary to be able to say, 'I can be at home with my family, and I can still keep my career.' They are so grateful for anything that they devalue their worth.

"I'll tell you something," Smith continues. "I once said, 'I love hiring women four days a week because they actually will produce at least five days' worth of work for four days' worth of pay.' And I have done that. I used to say four days was so much better than three. Three becomes a part-time job. Four is a full-time job done in four days!"

During our conversation, Smith becomes aware of exactly what she was admitting to. "It's only now that I'm sitting here and talking to you that I realize the implications," she says. "I will say, in the end, that however grateful we are for the work, going in there, we women have to value ourselves higher."

Former CFTC chair Brooksley Born agrees that being a mother made her more efficient at work because she used her time more wisely and because working part-time kept her mind fresh: "I think that I certainly changed from being an employee without any responsibilities for children, who had the luxury of not being terribly efficient, to a mother who knew that every minute counted and I darn well better be concentrating. I think I became much more efficient, and it's helped me ever since."

Did Born overcompensate and work harder than she did as a full-time employee? "I don't think [that as a part-time worker I was contributing] 100 percent," she says, "but I do think that I was doing more than 50 percent of my full-time work." Born does feel, however, that being a mother helped her be more productive. "I, myself, felt that working three days a week, I could contribute something more in three days than I could when I was working five-and-a-half or six days a week. Partly because I had a lot more stamina, partly because when I was in the office, I wasn't making personal phone calls or going out to lunch, or you know, any of the frills. I was really working. I also found that there was an advantage, to me at least, when solving complex strategy issues or complex legal questions, in getting away from the office, being with the children. I would work Mondays, Wednesdays, and Fridays, and so I had days off in between days of work. I would often come back to the office, and somehow or other my subconscious had gone a long way toward solving the problems. The most difficult strategy problems had been worked out while I was at the playground."

Valerie Jarrett agrees that being a mother taught her new skills. "Having children teaches you a certain conscientiousness and discipline and responsibility," she says. "I think what women have to do, that we don't often do, is recognize those broader life experiences add value—they don't subtract."

Did the fact that she was a single mom, trying to balance everything, affect her perception of herself and what she had to offer?

Jarrett answers, "Yes, very much so. Part of what gave me the strength to leave [an early job at a law firm], quite frankly, was that I was not doing a very good job because I had no passion for what I was doing. I wanted my daughter to be proud of me, and I thought if I stayed on that track she wouldn't be. It wasn't just knowing that she was solely relying on me financially; she was solely relying on me as a parent. I remember looking at her and saying, 'You're all I have, and I've got to really do right by you.' So I think my daughter made me more ambitious and much more able to push myself, because I was pushing myself for her."

Daily Beast cofounder Tina Brown agrees that women will handicap themselves by always taking family into consideration. "There's no doubt having children makes you do a kind of instant review of any problem that comes up, or any challenge or any opportunity with regard to the children," she says. "Immediately you think, 'Will this job mean that I have to travel more? I can't.' 'Will this job mean I have to work so late at night that I miss dinner with the kids? No, I can't.' You're tortured about how you're going to confront it. And to be honest, a lot of men, most men I think, even now, won't even [take the family picture] into the consideration of their job. They'll simply say, 'That's a great opportunity. Yes!'"

Brown and I also talk about the fact that women don't feel they can put family concerns on the table without immediately losing value. Especially at the executive level, we "immediately downgrade ourselves" if we raise those issues at work.

And as a result, we're less likely to take the time we need to recover physically from having a child. Brown remembers, "I had just given birth to my second child, my daughter, Isabel, in 1990. It was exactly that time that Condé Nast decided they were going to launch *Vanity Fair* in the UK, which meant, I realized, that I was going to have to go to London."

She was nursing at the time, so did she take the baby with her? Leave her home? She says she was also "enormously overweight. I had just had a child, I did not want to be starting on the promotion circuit having just had a child. I did not want to be posing for glamour shots instead of being at home quietly." Ultimately Brown decided she couldn't say no, and she couldn't take the baby on this incredibly demanding trip, so she went alone, and "was secretly distraught the whole time."

Brown didn't feel that she could tell her bosses that she needed to accommodate her post-pregnancy body. "I knew that that date was going to collide, but I didn't have the confidence to say, 'I will do this better in September, not in March, when my body's ready.' It would not have occurred to me to bring up that question early in the planning. And I just don't know if anyone would have heard me anyway," she says.

Brown's story resonated deeply with me, because I rushed back to work after my second child, and I should not have. One day I had a horrific accident with her. Working overnights and running on two hours' sleep, I had her in my arms when I fell down a flight of stairs, and she broke her thigh bone. I lived through hell knowing that my baby suffered so much pain because I wasn't managing my time and my sleep well. The fact is we've got to listen to our bodies and have the confidence to say, "You know what? I'll be there when I'm ready."

That said, how many companies are really willing to wait? For many women, saying, "I'll be there when I'm ready" is the same as saying, "I quit." Companies don't always have the money or patience to accommodate us, and we know that.

Harvard director Victoria Budson says there are things you can do to prepare in the event you can't commit to full-time work right away. "If you are in a large company, for example, studies have shown that even if you are working only one day a month, or two days a month, or you keep one client relationship, continuing to maintain both the social network and the work connection to the office can be instrumental in helping you back to your full-time career with fewer repercussions. When women leave the workforce and take time off, they often are underemployed the rest of their lives. So maintaining a client connection and/or working with your office in some way can really mitigate that effect."

What if you can't keep one foot in your previous job? Budson suggests that you control your own story. "I think it can also be very constructive for women to very consciously build their work narrative, and to think about how they are going to describe their leave and their return, and to own the expertise they may have been developing while not in formal paid employment. If one is active on the board of a nonprofit, if one is doing volunteer work, for your building skills that you really talk this skill, because during project management whether it is for paid or not for paid, it is an important skill. Raising money is an important skill and not to devalue the work that you are doing just because it is not formal employment."

> *I think it can also be very constructive for women to very consciously build their work narrative.*
> —VICTORIA BUDSON

Throughout all of this, we can only control what we control, but one choice we can make is whether or not we work for family-friendly companies.

CBS's Norah O'Donnell notes that, "If you work for a good company, they're usually pretty understanding about it . . . [it's possible to find] male and female bosses who completely understand and are completely willing to work with you."

O'Donnell says that when she first started working in the Washington, D.C., bureau she was working seven days a week, filling in for whoever couldn't show up. "I was taking everybody's shift . . . anything to get on the air because I was a network correspondent at twenty-five, and I was lucky to be there. After a year or so I asked if I could have one day off. It was a weekend day, and I just wanted to get things done. I was told by the deputy bureau chief at that time, who was a woman, an unmarried woman without children, that if I ever asked for a day off again, I probably wouldn't get these assignments. What's fascinating is that it wasn't from a male boss. That was from a female boss, who I believe had been forced in a different era to make those concessions in order to get into a position of power, and she was just passing what she'd learned on to younger women."

O'Donnell also tells the story of how she felt tremendous guilt when she got pregnant with her third child, Riley, four and a half months after giving birth to twins, Henry and Grace. O'Donnell's babies were born a decade after mine, yet we felt the same stress about telling our bosses the news. We both worried it would diminish our value or even disappoint our bosses. In both cases we were wrong.

I was embarrassed to tell my boss, Tim Russert,
that I was pregnant again. —NORAH O'DONNELL

"I was this hard-charging correspondent who's been all around the world," O'Donnell tells me, "who is always gone on call 24/7 and gung ho." In her mid-thirties, she decided she wanted to have kids, so she took a new position as chief Washington correspondent. It was as demanding a job as any other, but it involved less travel. She soon gave birth to twins and felt that she was just getting her momentum back at work when she found out she was pregnant again. She was so embarrassed to tell her boss, NBC News's Washington bureau chief Tim Russert, that she put it off until there was no way to hide the evidence.

When O'Donnell finally did break the news, she realized she was lucky to be working for someone who valued family, and who also valued her as an employee. "I was so silly to have been embarrassed to tell him, because Tim was more than thrilled," she says. "He was so excited, in fact, that he suggested the name Riley, which is what I ended up naming my daughter."

I had a similar experience years ago, when I discovered I was pregnant with my first child, Emilie. I pained over how to tell my news director at WFSB Channel 3 in Hartford, Connecticut. But like Tim Russert, my boss, Mark Effron, was ecstatic for me, and even suggested my pregnancy would be great for ratings. My daughter was due in January, but he joked, "Any way you could hold out till the May ratings book?"

Obama advisor Valerie Jarrett tells a story about the moment she realized she was working for the right boss. She was working for Chicago Mayor Richard Daley as the Commissioner of Planning and Development. She and Susan Sher, who was the corporation counsel, had just taken their jobs and were in one of their first meetings with the mayor. "I don't even know what we were talking about," Jarrett says, "but Susan and I were sitting across from each other, and the mayor was at the head of the table. He could be a little intimidating. We keep looking at our watches, then looking at him, and he's talking and not paying much attention. Suddenly it dawns on him that we're not really 'in' the meeting—we're somewhere else. He pauses and says, 'What's going on? Clearly you guys have somewhere else you'd rather be, what's going on?' And in a moment of truth, Susan and I look at each other and make eye contact. I said to him, 'The Halloween parade starts in twenty minutes. Our kids are in the same class, and we've never missed a Halloween parade.' He pauses and says, 'Then why are you still sitting here?' It was like the weight of the world was lifted from our shoulders. We go racing down Lakeshore Drive and we get to our children's school literally as these two little darlings are coming out of school in their costumes, and of course the first thing our kids do is look for us. I can't tell you how many times we've said to each other, 'What were we doing sitting there when all we had to do was ask?'"

Jarrett says part of the life lesson there is you've got to stick up for what you need and what's important to you: "If he had said, 'Well, I'm sorry, but I need you to stay here,' then we were working for the wrong person," she tells me. "You shouldn't be afraid to find that out. [Michelle Obama] often tells the story about taking Sasha to a job interview because she couldn't find a babysitter, and she learned a lot about Mike Riordan, her boss, because it was fine with him. If it hadn't been fine with him . . . isn't it good to know that early?"

Those experiences have taught Jarrett to be a better boss: "I think as a manager I try to encourage women and men to feel empowered to ask for what they need. Everybody here has children and I'm always saying to them, 'Don't miss the Halloween parade.'" She says hard-working employees who are able to take a few hours off for personal issues are going to come back feeling terrific about their jobs, and they're going to continue giving their all.

Former Yahoo! CEO Carol Bartz echoes those sentiments. "One of the things I say to people who work for me is, 'Your child only has one Christmas pageant, only has one concert, and there will be a staff meeting until the end of eternity, so you know, don't miss that stuff.'"

Writer and former *Cosmopolitan* editor Kate White tells the story of leaving her job when she realized she was working for the wrong boss. She was in the number-two position at *Mademoiselle* when she had her first child. Her boss, a woman without kids, called her into her office a week after White had returned from maternity leave and told her she didn't want her leaving at 5:00 every day. White didn't feel comfortable pointing out that the boss herself left at 5:30 every day, and that White was putting in extra hours every day after the baby went to sleep. At that moment, she says, "I stepped back and thought, 'What's going to give me more control?' I realized being an editor-in-chief would do that. Working at a different type of magazine, such as a parenting magazine, would do that. When I heard about the job at *Child* opening up, I figured they don't want a bad mommy in that job. When I got to the third interview and they said, 'Do you have any other questions?' I leaned forward and I said, 'I'd just like to conclude by saying how much I'd love this job and I think I would be terrific at it, blah blah blah.' The publisher, who was a woman, later said that she loved that I asked for the job. I remember saying to my son Hunter later—even though he was a baby—lying on the bed with him, saying, 'You helped Mommy get a great job because you made me ferocious.'"

She adds, "I have to say, Mika, I think I did gravitate toward bosses who one, liked to give a long leash to their editors-in-chief, and two, understood being a working parent. So it was a combination. I was also lucky enough to be in a field where there's a lot of flexibility."

Ask Yourself the Hard Questions

Former director of the Domestic Policy Council and chair of the Aspen Institute's Forum for Community Solutions Melody Barnes is a perfect example of someone who has never shied away from the hard questions, and she knows how important they are to create a home situation that works best for you. While Melody does not have children, so much of her advice applies to anyone working to plan and have an open dialogue about their wants and expectations. With a career that has taken her from a Wall Street law firm to the White House, she has had to constantly take time to reassess her path. When I asked her how she managed to merge all the aspects of her life, she explains, "In my head, I envision a gate and the question I always ask myself is, 'Do I want to walk through that gate, does the choice I'm making further my essential goals and objectives? What matters to me? What has purpose for me? What's on mission for me?'"

Taking this time to step back and looking at the possible outcomes of her choices is a skill that Melody applies to both her personal and her professional life, allowing her to have both a successful career and a life at home.

"When my husband and I decided to move from Washington to Richmond, Virginia, that was a big decision and we went through a very intentional process. I laugh sometimes when I describe this to people, because I say it shows you how much my husband loves me; most men would run away from what I proposed. I said, 'This is what we're going to do; we're going to write individual mission statements. We're going to write a mission statement as a couple, as a family, and determine our purpose. What do we want our lives to look like, feel like, literally every day when we get up; [and later] when we are dead and gone, what do we want to leave behind?' My husband often calls it the 'if I get hit by a bus, have I left this place better than the way I found it' test. What is it that we would've left behind that makes us proud? In going through that process and talking about it, it helped us make a series of decisions that have felt really wonderful and right for us."

Taking the time to align her own goals with the objectives of her family allowed Melody the flexibility to make changes and pursue new opportunities. The framework for their family was already established, making it easier to make choices that fit within their plans.

Letting Go of the Guilt

Women's advocate Marie C. Wilson says, "Women who are coming up [the leadership] pipeline have to make really tough decisions about children and work, because as you and I know, those jobs are 24/7, so you really have to decide, is that the way you want to live? Sometimes women don't want to make those choices. I used to not believe this, but I think increasingly women are saying, 'Why would I want to live like that?' And more men are too, as a matter of fact."

Wilson believes that the problem is the sociocultural ideal of women in America has never changed. While many women work as executives, society still primarily thinks of them as wives and mothers. The result, Wilson tells me, is that "while there've been more companies that offer flexibility, which helps, there's not a real commitment to making sure that there's a national child-care policy, that there are ways that women can enter and re-enter the workforce at the same level if they leave to have children, that there's complete support for paternity leave," which would allow men to share family responsibilities equally.

> *Show me a woman without guilt and*
> *I'll show you a man.* —MARIE C. WILSON

Wilson agrees that one of the things that keeps women out of positions of power is that "they're not just having to negotiate at work; women have to negotiate at home if they are in a two-career household, which they usually are." How do they get enough support at home to be able to do a 24/7 job? "I've often said, 'Show me a woman without guilt and I'll show you a man,'" she says. "Because frankly, women end up feeling guilty at work because they are not doing enough at home and feeling guilty at home because they're not doing enough at work."

Host of MSNBC's *Your Business* and successful entrepreneur JJ Ramberg, also has the experience of a lot of things competing for her time. "I try to keep things in perspective. It's not a big decision you make one day about the rest of your life; I think it's a bunch of little decisions that you make every single day. You know sometimes I ask myself, if I look back on this in ten years, will I have wished I stayed at work to write an article for this magazine or will I wish that I had gone home to do something with my kids? And I think those are questions that you should ask yourself every single day, if you're in a position to do so."

Because she knows that the answers to these questions can change often.

"Life changes, people change, jobs change, kids change," and she learned this from her own mother.

Life changes, people change, jobs change,
kids change. —JJ RAMBERG

"I was very lucky; I had an amazing role model. My mother was fortunate enough to decide what she wanted to do when we were younger, and she didn't work. She did a lot, A LOT, of volunteer work. But she didn't have a paying job. And then when she was in her late forties, she started a company with my brother that she ran for thirteen years, and they ended up selling it to Monster.com. So I got to see a woman who had two very distinct chapters in her life and excelled in both of them. And I think she was equally respected, by all of us and by the world at large, in both chapters. . . . When suddenly she had a job, I wasn't like, "Oh, NOW she's amazing." I thought she was amazing both before and after, so I had a real role model for two very distinct paths."

JJ's mother taught her how you work, change your path, and still remain a whole version of yourself. As we think about the challenges of motherhood as we navigate the corporate ladder, it leads me to a deeper question: How can we become the version of ourselves that is whole when we are at work, as well as when we are at home? The answer is unapologetic honesty . . . and I learned that the hard way.

CHAPTER 9

LOOKS MATTER

Own Who You Are

My story, with Melody Barnes, Katty Kay, Susan Chira,
Kasie Hunt, Joe Scarborough, and Janine Driver

The "Facelift" Tweet

There was nothing unusual about that Thursday on the set of *Morning Joe*. Washington was gridlocked, the Trump White House was trolling the press, and I was having a little harmless fun at the expense of the president of the United States. After reading a news story about Donald Trump posting fake *Time* magazine covers on the walls of his country clubs, our staff decided to create a fake *GQ* article to poke fun at the bogus covers, and we were lightheartedly showing it on air.

Our mornings are regularly filled with critiques of the 45th president. We tackle the stream of bizarre tweets, his ill-conceived Muslim ban, and a thousand other rabbit trails that showman Trump sends down to the media mob every day. And while my cohost Joe Scarborough and I have long fallen far out of the president's favor, staff members at the White House told us he still regularly watches the show. Trump would often push back on our reports online, but rarely blasted us with personal attacks.

That changed quickly on the Thursday before the long Fourth of July weekend in 2017. Apparently, one of our jokes hit a nerve.

I was finishing the final segment of the show while Joe was off set calling his children, when I noticed everyone around me intensely hunching over their phones. Suddenly, there was a palpable feeling of tension on the set, so I turned to Willie Geist and asked, "What's going on?" He was reading his phone with it conveniently angled away from me, so that I couldn't view the offending content. After a decade with the same on-air team, I can tell you this was definitely not how we roll on the set.

Willie, caught off-guard and nervous, refusing to answer? Red flags flew up immediately. And then I heard Executive Producer Alex Korson's strained voice in my earpiece issuing his instructions from the control room. "Mika, do not move. Stay where you are. I am coming out to show you something. DO. NOT. MOVE."

Alex, Joe, or any other guy on the set knows that sending me orders or directives usually makes things more difficult for them. Regardless, I knew what was coming even before Alex reached the set.

"Willie, show me what he tweeted," I said to my protective cohost. Willie knew he had no choice but to hand over his phone. I let out a quiet laugh as I started to read.

8:52 AM: "I heard poorly rated @Morning_Joe speaks badly of me (don't watch anymore). Then how come low I.Q. Crazy Mika, along with Psycho Joe, came . . ."

I then let out a *loud* laugh. When you expect him to react with pettiness, Donald Trump rarely disappoints. His tweets were predictably childish, unpresidential. And they were packed with lies. While I expected no more from the man, everyone around the set looked nervous and on edge.

Then I read the next tweet:

8:58 AM: ". . . to Mar-a-Lago 3 nights in a row around New Year's Eve, and insisted on joining me. She was bleeding badly from a face-lift. I said no!"

Okay, this one seemed a little rougher—but only to the untrained eye. Joe and I have known Donald Trump for over a decade. As Joe had written during the height of the presidential campaign, the GOP nominee had all the discipline of a small puppy wetting on the floor. But silence filled the studio and my staff were now trying their best to avoid making eye contact with me, the face-shamed TV host.

Someone else in my position might have felt humiliated, but I just could not suppress my laughter. Everyone on the set exhaled, and we went to get Joe's take. As we raced down the stairs, we passed through our newsroom, where our team looked shocked and stricken. As Alex and I burst through our office door, Joe looked up while laughing and asked, "Twenty-fifth amendment, anyone?"

As usual, Joe and I were on the same page. After the joking abated, we found ourselves less concerned by personal slights than by the fact that such an unstable man was running America.

Not so long ago, being personally attacked online by the president of the United States might have shaken me up. But I was blessed to be my father's daughter. My father, Zbigniew Brzezinski, was National Security Advisor to President Jimmy Carter, and a formidable personality—we called him "Chief." And my mother is equally hardy. A few rude tweets somehow pale in comparison to being chased out of your country in the 1930s by Adolf Hitler's Nazi blitzkrieg. And even though I may not be as tough as my parents, these Trump tweets were little more than sound and fury, signifying nothing more than the smallness of the president's character. I was always taught that, more often than not, personal insults reveal far more about the character of the attacker than anything about you.

In this case, I was concerned that the president's fixation on our show could drive him to expose his worst instincts in such a way. Joe and I told him on air the next day that he should probably watch *Fox & Friends*, for the good of America. But even as the news of his Twitter attacks ricocheted across the globe in one headline after another, Trump failed in his attempt to embarrass me.

After all, tabloids have written a good bit about my private life over the past few years. And what flaws they didn't reveal, I've probably revealed myself. I try to speak candidly about my struggles in all of my books and at my conferences, so that women can learn how I have faced my challenges through the years. I want women to learn from my mistakes—all of them. I also want them to know that how they handle the challenges they face is up to them, and not anyone else. The last thing I would ever want to do is lie about what I have and have not done in fighting my body-image issues.

So, yes! I have had cosmetic surgery. I have to wake up at 4 AM *every day* and struggle to look as presentable as possible as a 50-year-old woman on unforgiving, high-definition television. I got what I called a "chin tuck" to get a little extra skin tightened under my chin. I shared all of this with my friends and family members. Joe always accuses me of oversharing the details, but I like to tell people close to me what is going on in my life. I guess I would have to actually be embarrassed about that small procedure in order to be properly "face-shamed" by the president, but I just wasn't. In fact, I was pretty darned happy with the results!

Still, there are times when I can be too open about such things. One of those times was (obviously) when the president-elect invited us to drop by Mar-a-Lago in late December 2016. The invitation itself would have been unthinkable a few months before. Joe and I had used our *Morning Joe* platform to level harsh criticism at the Trump campaign for most of the preceding year. After the election, Joe and I leveled the same criticisms on air as we did in person. And yet, despite our public conflicts, Trump would often call Joe to discuss the show and his new administration. Joe would use the opportunity to steer him away from his most unwise cabinet picks and inflammatory, racist policies. Trying to moderate his approach seemed like a worthy effort, but we knew from the start that trying to reason with Donald Trump was a losing battle; in the end, Trump is always a prisoner to his fragile ego.

On December 30, 2016, the president-elect invited me and Joe to have dinner with Melania and two of their friends. Joe politely declined because I had just gotten my procedure, and he didn't want to go without me. But Trump was insistent. High-ranking members of Trump's staff were also begging Joe to go that night because they wanted him to talk about the importance of having a more diverse cabinet—specifically suggesting a Latino business leader to run the Department of Veterans Affairs.

Joe reluctantly left his kids and me to sit down with the Trumps for dinner. Sitting next to Donald, Joe made his pitch for diversity and excused himself early. But not before the president-elect asked if I could come the next night to Mar-a-Lago. Joe said it was doubtful, but promised he would try. The next day, an insistent Donald called again, asking for me. Joe got off the phone and shook his head. "Man, that guy is *obsessed* with you."

"Well," I remember reluctantly responding, "maybe we can get an inaugural interview out of it." Even though I was feeling terrible, I knew I had no choice but to show up and use whatever opportunity I had to pitch the interview idea. I had once dragged myself onto a plane to Iowa in the winter of 2007 to interview Michelle Obama, despite dealing with excruciating pain from an abdominal surgery that should have kept me in bed for a week. But I had been a reporter for almost thirty years, and there are some leads you just do not pass up.

When we got to Mar-a-Lago on New Year's Eve, Trump's pre-party was in full swing on the front lawn. I had a fever and was not in the mood to wade through hundreds of Palm Beach partygoers decked out in formalwear, but we fought our way through and found the president-elect. He quickly took us up to his family quarters, where Melania was getting ready for the party.

Barron bounded in with a friend, and his father patiently put on his bow tie and playfully talked with him and his friend about golf. Melania came in and asked if I was feeling better. I said I was and explained in confidence that I had gotten some extra skin on my chin tightened. Donald immediately came over and started asking who my doctor was and was very interested in the subject of plastic surgery. (The doctor's name is Dr. Hass, for your information, Mr. President, if you ever consider doing more work). A few minutes later, I brought up the idea of an Inauguration Day interview, and then we were on our way out the back. Within thirty minutes, Joe and I were back in sweats at our friend's house. He watched *Ghostbusters* with his kids. I went to sleep. Little did I know that months later, after he became president, he would twist the events of that night in a flurry of tweets in a failed attempt to soothe his bruised ego.

But by the time Trump tweeted that I was "bleeding badly from a face-lift," I was already preoccupied with more significant events in my life. It had been only a month since the death of my father, and I was still processing his passing.

My father's death was only the latest in a string of emotionally exhausting events that had hit me over the prior few months. My close friend Tia, after an agonizing two-and-a-half-year struggle, lost her achingly long battle with pancreatic cancer in March. And then in April,

Joe proposed, and I was engaged to be married. We were overjoyed. And in May, weeks before my father died, on the very day I found out he had had a stroke, I had the scare of my life when someone stole my daughter Emilie's phone and called in a bomb threat with it. She doesn't want me to reveal the details, but there were a few agonizing hours when I thought she had been kidnapped and there was a mass search underway. Once that nightmare was resolved, I rushed to Fairfax Hospital so I could be at my dying father's bedside.

Life was coming at me in such a blur, I felt broken and dizzy. My father would struggle for the next few weeks before passing away peacefully, with his wife of sixty-three years, his two boys, and his frazzled, adoring daughter at his side. My father's passing pulled me, Mark, Ian, and my mom together in a way he had always wanted. But my mother's heart literally broke, and she suffered two heart attacks the week after he died. My brothers and I orchestrated his funeral while she remained in the ICU. For weeks after his death, we were grieving while also managing care for an eighty-five-year-old artist who wields a chainsaw and works on pieces that weigh several tons and are two stories high (let's just say she does not accept "care" easily).

I found myself squeezed in the "supersized sandwich generation" of life's challenges—managing aging parents, supporting two college kids, juggling a full-time job with long hours, coping with a divorce, and considering how to balance all of that and handle the details of a complicated, public second marriage in the future.

I say this all to show why a tweet from Trump just seemed like nothing. NOTHING. I had been through an emotional roller coaster for four months (plus I did actually have the surgery), so why would this hurt me? A few vindictive tweets just seemed so small.

Having said that, PEOPLE WERE FREAKING OUT ABOUT THE TWEETS!

I realized quickly that the people who make *Morning Joe* possible—our staff, my cohosts, and the network—took this very seriously.

They, and I think specifically the women in my office, were upset on my behalf. They looked stricken. I heard from my female friends and colleagues who couldn't believe I was mocked by a president acting like a third-grade schoolyard bully.

It seemed the entire world was outraged, phones were ringing off the hook in the newsrooms, cell phones were exploding with texts, emails, and calls. I wanted everyone to know I was okay—because I was! But this did not appear to be okay to the rest of the universe.

From Democrats to Republicans to Hollywood, and even to people just tuned into Trump, this was *so* not okay!

Joe and Alex sat with me, fielding phone calls, as we discussed how to handle this. Should I respond? Should the network? Lorie Acio from public relations started calling with her insights, and senior vice president of communications at NBCUniversal News Group, Mark Kornblau, was preparing to tweet out a formal statement from NBC. They all were holding emergency conference calls and were very concerned about me. The atmosphere was "Code Red" all over the building. I wondered if the sprinklers would start going off and we would have to evacuate. It felt like that. Like chaos, war, total panic.

I think that was when it dawned on me: The president of the United States just tweeted this. Even after everything that had happened over the last two years, I still thought of him as a man who I had known for years. Someone who I had once been friends with but no longer respected. Someone who I expected to react explosively and hit below the belt. But this wasn't just an insulting tweet from eccentric billionaire and fellow NBC employee, reality-show star Donald Trump. This was a classless, misogynistic show of vulgarity from the leader of the free world. How sad for America, how embarrassing for us. People were upset for me. I started to get upset that our president was so small, so petty, so easily played.

There I was, sitting in my office, phones ringing off the hook around me, everyone wondering what to do next.

Mark Kornblau was on speaker. Alex and Joe were huddled around me at our desk. We were debating a response. I really didn't feel that one was needed. Until . . . Alex motioned to the breakfast that the interns always leave in my office for us to wolf down during our 8 AM break. He was focused on my Cheerios box. Specifically the image on the back of the box: two baby hands and the slogan, "Made for tiny hands."

I like to consider this Alex Korson's finest hour. He pointed at the image and said in a careful, measured voice, "Maybe just tweet a picture of that?"

YES. Joe was laughing, "Absolutely!" and the clincher was Kornblau.

Mr. "Let's Play It Safe" himself. This is a man who methodically strategizes all communications with the mindset of how one wrong letter could impact you ten months down the road. Mr. "Hold-on-now. Let's-look-at-the-possible-consequences" Kornblau. Yeah—that guy. The one who always checks with the network brass first.

He was an absolute *yes* as well.

He didn't even stop to think, or get clearance from NBC. Over the speakerphone, he blurted, "Oh wow, that's awesome. How quickly can you get that out?"

I was already typing.

The tweet was going out.

The best response to presidential "face shaming" would have to be humor.

That was my response. I thought it was flip, funny, and the end of that conversation. But I could not have guessed the reaction that came next.

My Cheerios tweet was retweeted, liked, shared, and used in articles across the country and the world—General Mills, you owe me! It quickly garnered international attention. (*My chin tweak getting international attention?*) Women whom I looked up to were sharing statements of support, and politicians on both sides of the aisle and on the global level were going on record to publicly denounce Trump's tweet.

I immediately became a sympathetic character on the world stage. For the first time in my entire life, I saw myself being painted as the victim. Up to this point, I don't think anyone would make the case that I was to be pitied in the media. I would say the positive accolade I hear the most is "strong." The majority of the opinions you will read in articles about me personally or professionally are polarizing. I can't think of a single time—ever—when the universal emotion was, "Wow . . . I feel so bad for Mika." How did we get here?

It Was About Something Bigger

I think the reason Trump's tweet sparked such a reaction is because he attacked my looks as a way of disqualifying my opinions.

These days, in Trump's America, sexism, misogyny, and the value of women seem to take center stage in every news cycle. His "locker room talk" was crude and childlike when he lived outside the White House, but his attitude was consistent with a coarsened popular culture populated by Paris Hilton, beauty pageants, and reality TV shows. Donald Trump, the actor and business mogul, was a guy who ran beauty pageants in questionable ways, made lewd comments about "grabbing women by the p**sy," and, in my experience and that of others, obsesses constantly over females and blood. He was an outlandish caricature whom you could avoid by changing the channel. But that was then. This is now. Now we have the president of the United States, whose words and actions inside the Oval Office have proven to be an affront to women.

How should we react when this kind of sexist behavior is condoned by *the president of the United States*? For so many of us, the fact that someone with such a low opinion of women could be acceptable to mainstream America was a rude wake-up call. (As disgusting as the man is, you have to admit, he's done a magnificent job of reinvigorating the Women's Movement.)

The election of Donald Trump shook millions of women out of their complacency. While a surprising 53 percent of white women voted for him, the day after his inauguration, an extraordinary number participated in the Women's March, one of the largest demonstrations in American history. The March brought together hundreds of thousands of women (and men) from across the country, many wearing pink pussy hats and carrying signs, protesting Trump's proposed policies against women, immigrants, and human rights in general. A new era of activism had suddenly dawned.

In this highly charged atmosphere, feminist movements from #TimesUp to #MeToo are spreading like wildfire. Incensed and inspired, more women are coming forward than ever before to run for public office. According to the Center for American Women and Politics at Rutgers University, at least seventy-nine women are exploring runs for governor in 2018, potentially doubling a record for female candidates set in 1994. Since President Trump's election, more than 26,000 women have reached out to Emily's List, which recruits and trains pro-choice Democratic women about running for office, about launching a campaign, according to *Time* magazine. This was up from only 900 between 2015 and 2016.

But even with the Women's Movement growing and strengthening around us, let's not kid ourselves—we all know women are still judged harshly for their appearances. Even if we have never entered a beauty contest before, women like you and me have been judged under the harshest of standards because of our faces, smiles, makeup, hair, legs, and other body parts that need not be mentioned in this space. Even after making it to a top national news network, I still find myself haunted by personal insecurities that date all the way back to those hours I spent in front of my bathroom mirror trying to look half as good as the pretty girls who seemed to breeze through my middle school, high school, and college classes, and later the local and national TV newsrooms. Even now when I do Facebook Live broadcasts with my chickens and rabbits, my comment feed will be bombarded with viewers telling me how ugly I am without makeup covering my face. (If that is the worst insult someone can dredge up about me, though, I'm doing pretty well—I learned a long time ago that neither you nor I have to look like a supermodel to achieve super success.)

Joe's experience working with me has led him to believe that women face far more difficult challenges over the long run than just voting in candidates who understand and champion women's issues.

"When I first started working with you, Mika, I was shocked by the angry, sexist attacks that you had to sort through every day on social media and in the comments sections of blogs," he said. Men were either demeaning my looks or offering lewd commentary. Meanwhile, Joe's audience "would just joke about how my hair looked like I had rolled out of bed and went straight to the studio. Because that was usually true . . . but the imbalance in reactions between a male and female cohost was shocking." Joe also noted that in our decade together, his weight has fluctuated by as much as thirty pounds, and yet no one ever seems to take note of his weight or appearance except on his "very worst days." And yet, he continues, "If you pick up five pounds, someone will immediately comment that you need to go on a diet. If you lose five pounds, you will get attacked for being too skinny and unhealthy. And if your makeup is a little bit off in the eyes of the viewers, the comments will flood in like a waterfall. It is a no-win situation when it comes to being a woman on TV dealing with her looks. The judgment is always going on, and it is usually harsh."

> *The judgment is always going on, and*
> *it is usually harsh.* —JOE SCARBOROUGH

Yes. At the age of fifty, I have, at this point, heard it all. It doesn't get easier, but as I have gotten older, things that matter have become clearer.

The fact is this: however much we'd like to think looks don't matter, they do. Especially for women. However much we'd like to think that our culture has evolved, that how a woman looks has no bearing on her success or failure at work, and that colleagues are obligated by common sense, a moral code, a code of business conduct, or actual law to treat female colleagues with due respect and equanimity, that's really just so much idealistic thinking. The way a woman looks affects the way she is treated, in ways that are both overt and covert, conscious and subconscious, every day.

The question is, how do we continue the battle for our value in this context? How can we keep pressing to be treated fairly, to get coworkers to judge us and other women by something more substantial than our looks?

Overt and Covert Aggressions

One way to combat the effects of "lookism"—discrimination based on a person's physical appearance—is simply to be vigilant. When women's looks matter more than they need to, and insults or admiration of women's looks actually interferes in the workplace, we need to acknowledge it, and speak up.

News headlines and public outrage are usually reserved for the type of attacks on women that are too outrageous to ignore. But even more prevalent is the subtle bias that women face because of their appearance—the countless insults that can reduce women to little more than sexual objects. As so many of my interviewees reminded me, the multitude of slights aimed at women in the workplace is just as important as the worst examples of sexism that make the front pages of newspapers. Think of it this way: mass shootings with military-style weapons may dominate America's newsrooms for weeks at a time, but the fact is, the overwhelming majority of gun-related deaths are from individual handgun shootings that happen every day. The shocking stories may grab the headlines, but it's the smaller, easily overlooked, but utterly pervasive acts that do the most lasting damage.

Katty Kay is a presenter for *BBC World News America*, a best-selling author, and a regular contributor on *Morning Joe*. She also happens to be a close friend and is one of the fiercest fighters for women with whom I have ever had the pleasure of working. Case in point: that infamous *Morning Joe* interview when she asked future Secretary of Housing and Urban Development Ben Carson about Trump's alleged sexual harassment, and when she pressed him for a straight answer, he suggested that Joe turn off her microphone. She said Carson "passed it off as a joke. But it wasn't. It's that constant belittling of women, disguised as humor, that creates a culture where it's okay to undermine women's abilities."

And don't get her started on the face-lift tweet.

"It was a classic case of someone putting the focus on a woman's physical appearance in order to get people not to focus on her talents," Katty said. "When something like that happens, we must all speak out together. I remember many saying that women in the White House should have condemned the behavior, that's true, but men should just as much. Stopping this kind of sexism isn't just our responsibility."

> *When something like that happens,*
> *we must all speak out together.* —KATTY KAY

The New Normal Isn't Normal

I remember being fired by CBS News in one of the most shocking chapters of my entire career. When pressed for a reason why one of the key players in management wanted me gone, the only answer I got back was, "He thinks you look weird."

It was a jarring comment, but in time, that insult motivated me to ensure some man's subjective feelings about my facial structure would never play a factor in my future career again.

Many of my colleagues on TV know all too well what it is like to have their worth be summed up in a sentence or two about their looks, and I think the reason so many people reached out after the face-lift tweet is that what happened to me felt familiar to women of all walks of life.

You don't need to be a cable news talk show host to experience these types of comments; they happen to all of us, all the time. They happen when men yell out the window at women walking down the street. They happen when coworkers feel like they have the right to comment on how you look—Every. Single. Day. I think part of the reason that so many women were quick to jump to my defense stemmed from all of our frustration with a climate where it is acceptable for women to be talked about as if they have no value. And if the leader of the free world can do it, what is to stop our bosses, our neighbors, our husbands?

I expressed my frustration about this to President Obama's director for the Domestic Policy Council, Melody Barnes: how can we tell young women to reach for the stars when they are hearing this type of language about women from men in power? She agreed that we are seeing an increased number of people who feel comfortable saying disparaging things about women. In the past, people might have thought the same things, but were discouraged by social norms from making sexist comments. "But now we're cultivating an environment where it's okay, and it's popping up everywhere."

Melody elaborates, saying that Donald Trump's tweets "let us know what many people have been thinking, and they also tell us what people are now comfortable saying, publicly, and we have to make that 'not okay.' We have to push back on that being our new normal—part of our workplace and cultural dialogue . . . there can't be a place where that's right."

Putting it simply, Melody says, "You can't stand on the sidelines when you see or hear something inappropriate . . . if you hear something, say something."

You can't stand on the sidelines when
you see or hear something inappropriate . . .
if you hear something, say something.
—MELODY BARNES

The *New York Times'* Susan Chira describes some of the shifts she observed during the 2016 election. "These kinds of comments on women's appearance were something that were thought of as relics of a past before feminism raised people's consciousness—that women shouldn't be evaluated on appearances; they should be evaluated as men are, on performance and competence. Focusing on their physical attractiveness is a way of demeaning them."

During the election cycle, Susan observed anger was a common theme, particularly among members of the working class who felt undermined and treated with disrespect. She noted "a lot of pent-up resentment about the way that working class people were portrayed," and sees the open antagonism toward women as something of "a punch-back."

No matter what side you're on, Susan reminds us that language matters. "It is really about what I consider to be basic standards of decency and dignity that should be applied to everyone—men, women, people of color, you name it. This applies broadly. I think we have to think hard about how we respond when someone makes a demeaning comment." In a perfect world, Susan says, civil discourse would be characterized by "decency, dignity, respectful dialogue, and respectful disagreements." However, we're living in a climate where opinions have become progressively more polarized, and the cultural climate more divisive.

My fellow broadcast journalist and MSNBC colleague, Kasie Hunt, commented on the shift in tone as well when we sat down to speak for this book. She says, "I think one of the things that has changed the most under this president is the normalizing of all kinds of things that used to be essentially verboten in the public square. It's white supremacists being willing to do interviews without masks on, or openly stating their identities, or just using words that are crude, frankly."

So what can we do about it? Kasie suggests, "Saying what it is. Pointing out [open prejudice and antagonistic language], acknowledging it, and then not engaging in it is the way to move forward."

Acknowledging it, and then not engaging in it
is the way to move forward. —KASIE HUNT

Rise Above It

We can call out looks-ism—and then we can rise above it.

The most powerful tool you have at your disposal is *you*. Your story. Your passions, your pain, and your vulnerabilities. But most importantly, your talent.

NBC News reporter Katy Tur offers a great example of turning the conversation away from your looks and toward your talent. Ironically, it was her coverage of the 2016 Trump campaign that both brought her appearance to center stage, and also helped her move past it.

"Before I started doing politics, before I got into covering Trump on the campaign trail, when I would do a story—no matter what the story was—almost all the responses had something to do with my looks. I reported a story out of Louisiana on a brain-eating amoeba that killed someone and the first reaction I got back on Twitter was, 'Nice story about the brain-eating amoeba. You looked hot!'"

Her first sit-down with President Trump at Trump Tower in 2015 was the interview that catapulted her into being a prominent player in the election cycle. His annoyance at her questions and the way he belittled her actually worked in her favor, and struck a chord with viewers.

Remembering that encounter, she explains, "When I did that first Trump interview in July of 2015, I got a ton of tweets and a lot of attention on social media for the tough back-and-forth I had with the candidate. And yet, for the first time, not one of them had anything to do with my looks or the fact that I was a woman. The realization that all the discussion centered around the substance of the interview, and not my looks, was a real turning point for my career."

As the campaign wore on, like many journalists, Katy found herself on the receiving end of Trump's attacks. One of the many times he called her out specifically during a rally, the fury of the crowd turned so harsh that the secret service had to escort her to her car. Trump tried to demean her by calling her "Little Katy" and insulted her by saying she was a "third-rate reporter."

But unlike many women who consider Trump's ascendance a professional setback, Katy says the opportunity to display grace under fire earned her recognition for her work as a journalist, rather than as an attractive woman.

One of my favorite stories about combating bias about your looks comes from chief operating officer for the Mortgage Bankers Association, Marcia Davies. She managed to move the conversation past her appearance by demonstrating her *lack* of talent. "When I was younger in my career and one of the only senior female leaders in my company, I was asked to 'represent' the organization at a charity golf event with a few famous Washington, D.C., men. I was new to the game of golf, and I was asked to play with men who had low handicaps, so my confidence was shaky.

"I wanted to feel like my 'best self' in that situation, so I went out and bought a great new golf outfit that reflected a professional, very styled look. When I was introduced to the members in my foursome, the first thing one of them said to me was, 'Wow. Our team is going to win. You have a body made for golf, and I can tell by the way you are dressed, you play often.' He was so frustrated—and frankly quite angry—when I started to play and he realized there was no way our foursome would win the event. To this day, when I think of that interaction, it makes me smile."

Shelley Zalis, CEO of The Female Quotient, responds to negative comments by flipping the script to turn it into something positive. "I was on tour with the Voices of Veterans Tour, and young girls were helping to design prosthetic arms and legs made specifically for women (most prosthetics are designed one-size-fits-all). While we were on tour, a Nobel Laureate made a statement that men and women should not work together in the lab because women were distractingly sexy.

"What kind of a message is this for girls looking to get into STEM? So we created a T-shirt for us to wear that read #distractinglysmart. It turned the negative conversation into a positive moment in the girls' lives, and gave them confidence."

If there is one thing that we have learned throughout the rise of the Women's Movement, it's the power of social media and a great hashtag.

And that was not the only time Shelley put someone in his place when he tried to define her by her looks. She tells me, "Early in my career, I brought in a big piece of business for my company. My male boss at the time said, 'The only reason you got that business is because the client thought you were attractive.' I responded with, 'That may be how *you* do business, but I'm quite talented.' Whether he was kidding or not, I let him know it was offensive and he never said anything like that to me again. Find your voice, shut it down, and start a new conversation. Don't assume the other person knows they're making you uncomfortable; speak up and make them aware."

Find your voice, shut it down, and
start a new conversation. —SHELLEY ZALIS

Learning to Be Self-Possessed

Let's be honest: sometimes you will get extra attention as a female. The question is, how do you make sure the attention you're getting is a *good* thing? One of the issues we talk about at my Know Your Value conferences is how to own your physical presentation and work to command respect by your very presence. How to be self-possessed; what that feels like and looks like. Because putting yourself out there—whether you're attracting attention to your ideas by using your voice, raising your hand, or simply being physically present—is important.

Knowing your value means more than just knowing what your salary should be. It means having confidence in what you can do and who you are. In regard to your looks, it means developing composure—a sense of calm self-assuredness you express with your physical presence. It means owning your face, your voice, your eyes, your body, and your style in its true, authentic form. Great eye contact, posture, and a strong voice can come from any woman of any size, height, color, or appearance. The woman who owns her own voice and posture *can* own the room. And our concerns about not looking like supermodels or twenty-five-year-old reality stars or Miss America should stay out of our professional lives. Those fears and concerns cost us a lot of money. They get in the way of our message. You will lose in the long run if you measure your value by your looks because you will miss the opportunities to develop all your tools and skills. Looks do not replace talent and composure in the long run.

While it may not be fair, you should always be thinking about your professional appearance. Your clothes help form the first impression, so make sure you are sending the right message. *Fortune* assistant managing editor, Leigh Gallagher, suggests that when deciding what to wear for a workplace event, consider whether your clothes are helping to communicate who you are, or whether they're distracting. She tells me, "I happen to like form-fitting clothes. I always have. But as

I advanced in my career, I started to become aware that it wasn't always called for, and could sometimes be doing me a disservice. I once bought a great teal Hervé Léger bandage dress at a vintage store (I later learned it was fake, but it was a great fake!). When I was considering what to wear to a big journalism event at that time, I contacted the friend who had urged me to buy it—a respected investigative journalist and author. I asked her if she thought I should wear the dress to the event. She said, 'Here's the thing. You can wear that dress and you will look great. But you don't *need* that.' Her point? I didn't need to play the looks card; why take any attention away from my credibility? She was right."

Here is my take on dressing for success: Your goal should always be to feel comfortable and confident at work, and that means taking an extra beat to think about whether your clothes match your personal brand. There is a time and a place for everything, and Leigh's friend helped remind her that maybe the dress, which fit her body so well, didn't necessarily fit how she wanted to be perceived in this particular context. I have given similar advice to many, many women . . . including Leigh Gallagher herself.

She remembers, "You gave me some great advice early on when I started going on *Morning Joe*. I would wear form-fitting dresses in bright colors—what I saw other women on TV wearing, and what was the standard. You gave me different advice: you encouraged me not to try to look like a TV anchor, but instead dress like a journalist. Wear skinny jeans and boots and a crisp white Oxford and a chunky watch . . . roll up my sleeves. Look great and sharp, but double down on what I do—look like the working journalist that I am, rather than trying to look like a television anchor. It was great advice and, while you can certainly still see me in the occasional form-fitting outfit, I try to follow it to this day."

My point is, you can be yourself, feel amazing, and remain professional. When you do find an outfit that works, don't be afraid to wear it often. As Female Quotient CEO Shelley Zalis told me, "When you get dressed, dress in something you feel really good in, even if it is wearing the same thing over and over. If you feel good in that, then you will project yourself in a completely different way."

> *When you get dressed, dress in something you feel*
> *really good in, even if it is wearing the same thing*
> *over and over.* —SHELLEY ZALIS

Don't Be Afraid to Use Your Body Language

It's one thing to be comfortable in your clothes, but it's another to be comfortable in your own skin.

Like Shelley Zalis, Janine Driver is in huge demand to speak at conferences and events. The CEO of the Body Language Institute, Janine is a leading expert in the field of body language. For over a decade, Janine worked for the Bureau of Alcohol, Tobacco, Firearms, and Explosives (ATF), training thousands of the most elite law enforcement officers from all over the world to differentiate lies from the truth using proven body language interpretation methods. She went on to be an acclaimed coach, TEDx presenter, and author of the *New York Times* bestseller, *You Say More Than You Think: A 7-Day Plan for Using the New Body Language to Get What You Want.*

We asked her to join our Know Your Value event in October 2017 because she has important insight into how your thoughts affect your body language, and what your body language is saying to the people around you. Talk about owning a room—Janine blew us away! She had us laughing hysterically, waving our arms, shimmying, and crying our eyes out—then laughing again. Go look at her. (I can wait while you go to knowyourvalue.com.) Isn't she fabulous? Notice how confident her stance is. Look at how deliberate her physical actions are. She's incredible. Stay with me here, because I know you want to go back and watch more Janine.

Here is my point: she was overweight. She's a food addict, and she's worried that we may notice that. She's also scared. We talked about all these things for this book. Yes, a woman who has gone toe-to-toe with gun traffickers and bomb-makers was scared to death to face a crowd of women. She remembers her rising anxiety: "I am sharing the stage with Sarah Jessica Parker, Martha Stewart, Mika Brzezinski . . . seriously? C'mon. And I am a nobody. No one knows who the hell I am."

But Janine knew that she had to calm herself, or her body would reflect her anxiety. So as she was getting ready to own the stage, she sent her manager a text. "I wrote: I am value. I am power. I am kind. So when you were introducing me, I simply just thought of that text. I am value. I am power. I am kind."

Janine reminds me that you can defuse a moment of insecurity by simply acknowledging it. "Notice it . . . be mindful and say, 'You know what, STOP.'"

Then Janine stepped on the stage and proceeded to blow us away. Afterward, a woman from North Carolina came up to her and said, "I came here to see Sarah Jessica Parker, and I have never heard of you, but you ended up being the person I was here to see."

But for many of us, affirmations are not enough to get us to take that step forward and announce our values. Janine has advice about owning a room and your looks by explaining that, while all the women who graced the stage at our event were rock stars in their own right, the unique message you have to tell can resonate uniquely with different women . . . or not at all.

We are all, thank goodness, born looking different. Many of the things that make up our physical appearance are things completely out of our control, and stressing about the things that make you uniquely you is unproductive and unnecessary. I encourage women to lean in to their authentic selves, and that applies to your looks. But body language is that part of your physical appearance that *you can control*. You are in charge. You are driving the car. Own this power and make it work for you. The way that you carry yourself can change opinions, get you in the door, and change the tone of the conversation.

I have always known this, but Janine really drives the message home. This woman who struggles with her weight and self-doubt carries herself with a confidence and joy that makes her stand out in a crowd. Women were coming up to me after the event, wanting to hear more from and about Janine Driver. And that was because her body language, which she has complete control of at all times, made her one of the highlights of a star-studded event. She was stunning.

Janine knows looks matter, that's why she owns that stage. She commands respect with her posture and her voice and her humor, and within seconds, we literally are drawn in. One of my favorite pieces of advice she gave to me when we spoke came from her mother. She says, "Body language is great. I think of it like an oak tree. My mother, when she was fighting cancer, she used to hug an oak tree in the backyard and say, 'I'm like this oak tree—my roots go deep and I am strong.' And so I think like the oak tree. The roots of the tree are your intentions or your why. That comes first. Then comes body language."

Janine and I became instant friends. We plan to work together on a number of upcoming projects. We "clicked" because we both know the secret to owning a room and we are woman enough to want to share that talent with as many women as we can reach.

I speak at my events and on our website about posture, body language, and voice. These are your tools. Own them. Practice speaking in public. Look at what works for you and what doesn't. If you have no opportunity to speak in public, find one. Read at church, make a toast at an event. Have a party and make a speech about why you love your dog. *Put yourself out there.* Practice. And there is always your phone.

Hold it up in selfie mode and pitch yourself to one of our competitions. Show it to someone you respect. What works, what doesn't. Ask yourself why. Dig deep. Find your voice, connect with your eyes. Own your message. Your looks will transform and you will, too. There is no time to waste.

CHAPTER 10

#METOO AT WORK

So there I was on Thursday, October 5, 2017, the day that the Harvey Weinstein story broke on the front page of the *New York Times*.

HARVEY WEINSTEIN PAID OFF SEXUAL HARASSMENT ACCUSERS

FOR DECADES

It was the biggest news story of the day, one that would snowball into one of the biggest news stories of the year. Famous women's names were attached to it: Ashley Judd, Rose McGowan. His former employees, along with many others who chose to stay anonymous.

But while the world was glued to the reports with horrified fascination, I could not have been more out of it. I was completely disconnected from all the breaking news; I had taken the day off and driven my pickup truck four hours to Hanover, New Hampshire.

My daughter Carlie had been searching for an off-campus apartment for six months. Apparently, one can get housing in New York City faster (and cheaper) than in the vicinity of the Dartmouth College campus. Carlie needed a place where she could have her dog, Hobson, with her. Hobson is a HUGE Bernedoodle who turned out to be as big as Marmaduke . . . maybe even bigger.

As a mom, my gut told me Carlie needed Hobson as she adjusted to life away from home. And I won't lie, my household needed Carlie to have Hobson. Carlie had called me in a panic a few days earlier because she had found the perfect place, but we needed to act quickly. I took the day off from *Morning Joe* and raced up to help her move. In those twenty-four hours, we cleaned the new place, loaded up her old room, and drove everything to the apartment to unload it all.

I found a great furniture place and negotiated for a couch, bed, coffee tables, and lamps. Along with two nice gentlemen, I loaded up the truck. It was a backbreaking day. I even Instagrammed myself bleary-eyed in the back of the truck with the furniture. I was drenched in sweat, no makeup, but I had that "Mom is here to help" good feeling all over me. Carlie's place looked perfect by the end of the day.

I made the drive back to New York extremely late, completely oblivious to the massive news story that the country was responding to in real time. I woke up Friday morning to the news about Harvey, astounded. I wasn't ready to talk about it on the air. We did a segment on the story at the end of our show, but I held my fire.

I knew that I needed to really read it. The story was big and it needed my careful attention ASAP.

I spent that Friday reading all about what he did. I started direct-messaging with Ashley Judd on Twitter. I started thinking about the few times I ever had any type of contact with Harvey Weinstein over the years, and I was extremely uncomfortable with what I was remembering.

No, he never harassed me. In fact, he has invited Joe and me to countless events, and we almost always said no. We do not go out late, and his events were almost always in the evening. An evening event that would exhaust us had to be worth it, and the events Harvey invited us to never were.

But he was my book publisher.

With all of my book deals with Weinstein Books (I had published four titles with them at that point), I would hear, "Harvey wants to announce this right away!" Harvey always made a lot of noise about our publishing projects, which at the time seemed like a good thing. But my books have all been geared towards women, balance, health, and empowerment, and Harvey's extreme interest in them always struck me as strange.

I felt weird about Harvey. I know now that I am not alone in that feeling. But he was the Hollywood mogul whose name was on the publishing company, and the publishing executives always seemed so happy that Harvey would take a strong interest in my books and the announcement of them. No one had a problem with it in the past, so I didn't either.

When I negotiated a three-book deal with Hachette in September 2017, I was excited to update this book and introduce two new writers into the Know Your Value program.

Daniela Pierre-Bravo would coauthor a book with me on the challenge millennials face in this ever-changing, multi-generational workforce. My sister-in-law Ginny Brzezinski and I would retrace our separate career paths. We planned to address the challenges women face making career comebacks after taking time off. All three of these books were the next step for me in bringing the Know Your Value message to every woman who wants and needs to get value back in every relationship in their lives. First up would be this rerelease of *Knowing Your Value*.

Though I was so excited to negotiate this three-book deal, I was told, once again, before the contracts were even signed, "Harvey wants to leak this to Page 6." I was not ready. My coauthors hadn't even heard the news. And yet, the next day—without my permission—a blaring headline appeared in the *New York Post*.

MIKA BRZEZINSKI LANDS

"MEGA 3 BOOK DEAL WITH WEINSTEIN BOOKS"

Huh?

The deal was three books, yes. "Mega?" NO! It was enough to compensate my coauthors, pay for an editor, and while it was certainly "mega" to me because I know how valuable these books will be for so many women, it was not "mega-money." So why was Harvey so intent on making it look like . . .

Wait a minute . . .

On that Friday, when I first learned the news, I was pondering all of this—and then it hit me. Harvey liked using my books as a way to cover himself, to make it look like he cared about the value of women. He wanted the world to think he compensates authors generously who write about female empowerment and leveling the playing field. To me, there could be no other explanation for the exaggerated headline and his zeal to "break the news" about my book deal. I felt used, and I knew how impossible this relationship would be.

I knew I had already missed a news cycle, because of my mom trip to Dartmouth . . . I knew that left me with no time at all to respond. So I got on the phone. I studied. I reached out to as many women as I could who worked with Harvey, and finally collapsed that Friday night feeling all wrong about everything. I was also overwhelmingly tired from the long drive home and getting up at 4 AM to do the show.

Saturday morning I lurched awake. Joe is always up early on Saturdays to get my coffee, so he was just walking back in the door.

"I have to tweet now!" I screamed at him. I was fumbling all over the bed for my phone and racing through my mind was:

"MUST TWEET!"

"PUSH BACK IN REAL TIME!"

"What did your chickens do now?" Joe asked me half-jokingly. (I often Instagram and tweet about my hens.) Joe became concerned, watching me crawl around on the bed hunting for my phone.

"Mika, are you okay?"

"No! My book deal! It's done. I'm out." I am on the floor now in my pajamas, but no glasses as I flapped my hands all over the rug feeling for the phone.

Like an addict who just dropped her pill bottle. Must. Find. My. Phone.

Joe convinced me to sit back and drink a sip of coffee and talk it through, but before long he was right there with me on what to do.

I needed to respond in real time and I was already late.

At 7:42 AM, I tweeted:

"Harvey Weinstein needs to resign from his companies, face his sickness, and go into a long, self-imposed exile."

And at 7:46 AM, I tweeted again:

"Authors, actors, and moviemakers should not work for any Weinstein company until he resigns. Not a close call. #knowyourvalue"

And finally at 8:03 AM , I tweeted:

"I have a three-book deal with Weinstein Books, through Hachette. I can't go forward with those books unless Harvey resigns."

Within minutes, there was a waterfall of reactions. This part I did not expect. I just wanted to get on the record fast. I wanted to push back publicly in real time and put money on it.

MIKA BRZEZINSKI WANTS OUT OF BOOK DEAL

UNLESS HARVEY WEINSTEIN RESIGNS

MIKA BRZEZINSKI 'CAN'T GO FORWARD' WITH WEINSTEIN BOOK DEAL

Morning Joe's MIKA BRZEZINSKI TO CANCEL BOOK DEAL
UNLESS WEINSTEIN RESIGNS

I was out of a deal, but it all finally, and very quickly, felt right. Maybe ten years ago, before my Know Your Value journey, I would have thought way too long about what to do. I might have worried about the short-term money loss. These days, the words come easily and the big picture is very clear. The decisions are fast, deliberate, and with conviction. And the results are always priceless.

I had very little communication with Amanda Murray and Georgina Levitt, my "team" at Hachette, before I sent out those tweets. And that was purposeful. This was about business, and there was absolutely nothing to discuss. Yes, I left them hanging while I waited. There was to be no deal, in any way, shape, or form, with Harvey's name attached to it. I made that clear on the air of *Morning Joe* the following Monday.

My Saturday morning hysteria was a gut instinct that I needed to act on. I rushed to Twitter like Donald Trump on a "fake news" tirade. When a woman pushes back in real time, it gets noticed. We need to develop the confidence to respond quickly, because so often we overthink, troubleshoot, and ultimately miss the moment. We miss the opportunities to stand up and push back, because we are so busy thinking about our weaknesses. I wanted to make it clear that I would not work with Harvey Weinstein and put money on it. I wanted to practice what I preach. This was a Know Your Value moment.

To be very clear, I would never compare myself to the brave women who spoke out against one of the most powerful men in Hollywood by telling their painful stories. But I saw the opportunity to put my money behind the movement to help force him out of power and show my support. I saw the opportunity to put my value toward something good.

Then the Harvey story began to unravel even faster than I thought possible.

By Sunday, October 8, Harvey Weinstein was fired by the board of his company.

The following Tuesday, thirteen more women were added to the list of accusers, including three who accused him of rape. That week, A-list celebrities like Gwyneth Paltrow, Cara Delevingne, and Angelina Jolie shared their own harassment experiences with Weinstein.

And it did not stop there. British actress Lysette Anthony accused him of rape. Actress Lupita Nyong'o described him trying to lure her to his bedroom under false pretenses. This list grew at an unbelievably horrifying rate. As I am writing this, an astounding *eighty* courageous women have come forward.

But changes started to happen. He was expelled from the Academy of Motion Picture Arts and Sciences. He was removed from the Producers Guild of America. The industry response was extraordinary, and the #MeToo movement was gaining momentum with every passing day.

While there were a number of people depending on me to get the deal back on the table, I thought about Joe and Willie during their first *Morning Joe* negotiations. They had waited. They didn't show up until they got everything they wanted. Then they waited some more to make sure it was exactly what they wanted.

What I really wanted was a complete separation from the name "Weinstein" and my book series. There was no reason for me to lurch. The best advice I ever got from an old friend was, "Be still." Amanda and Georgina were reaching out to me repeatedly on email, but I told them I was not ready to talk. It felt very unnatural, but I was following my own advice.

Women move forward too quickly in negotiations. Men wait for weeks, often months, to get a deal right. Women just want it done. We want our assurance as we vie for safety over risk. So I went against the grain and I waited.

And then something remarkable happened a few days later.

Lorie Acio from MSNBC Public Relations texted me the latest headline:

WEINSTEIN BOOKS IS SHUTTERED BY HACHETTE BOOK GROUP
(*The New Yorker*)

WEINSTEIN BOOKS IMPRINT AXED; HACHETTE TAKES PROJECTS, STAFF
(*Deadline*)

HARVEY WEINSTEIN'S HACHETTE IMPRINT IS SHUTTING DOWN
(*Huffington Post*)

Hachette Publishing Group officially and immediately severed ties with the Weinstein imprint. This was a bold move and exactly what I hoped would happen.

I got a phone call from the CEO of the Hachette Book Group, Michael Pietsch, who was in Germany attending the Frankfurt Book Fair. But he took the time to tell me that the separation was complete, that the imprint was no more, and the staff—and my books!—would have a new home at another imprint. He also wanted me to know that Hachette, a company that has 70 percent women, considered gender equality a priority. He hoped it would be good news for all of us. It was. It was indeed.

Holding your fire can be a valuable attribute at times, but not when the moment matters to your value or when your brand is in question. And DEFINITELY not when something is wrong. When you develop skills in this realm, your employers and partners will value and respect your ability to identify problems and respond effectively. They will give you more responsibility. Your judgment will gain respect. But you have to show that you can do this in the moment without taking too much time personalizing business decisions. It is called pushing back in real time.

The conversation did not stop with Harvey Weinstein—it emboldened women everywhere, on a national level, to speak their truth and it sparked a movement. #MeToo was born from the ashes of the Weinstein Empire, on the backs of brave women who were not afraid to step forward with their own history of sexual misconduct and abuse.

In the aftermath of Weinstein's downfall, women (and men) rose up in unprecedented numbers to protest sexual harassment, and the consequences were shockingly swift. Major public figures in entertainment from Kevin Spacey, Louis C.K., and James Franco, news legends including *Today*'s Matt Lauer and CBS's Charlie Rose, politicians like Alabama Senate candidate Roy Moore, and even the President himself all had women come forward with allegations. Even longtime contributors to *Morning Joe* were immediately dismissed when issues became known. The list is ongoing and shockingly long.

A new sensitivity swept the country and radically shifted the status quo. Preventing sexual harassment was no longer just about maintaining civility at work and giving women the respect that they are due; it was about dollars and cents—movie studios can't make money on a movie if the star is known as a sexual abuser. Women won't vote for a politician who has a history of trying to date underage girls. Suddenly the reality that women constitute 51 percent of the population and have significant financial and political and cultural leverage was felt . . . everywhere.

According to a CNBC All-American Survey conducted from December 10 to 13, 2017, with 800 adults nationwide, overall 19 percent of American adults said they have been victims of sexual harassment in the workplace. Among men, the figure was 10 percent, while among women it jumped to 27 percent. And while this percentage changed slightly across different studies, one thing was abundantly clear: This issue was real and it was not going anywhere.

Companies began putting extensive sexual background training into place and establishing strict sexual harassment policies. A January

2018 study from Challenger, Gray & Christmas (an outplacement services firm) reported that 48 percent of companies responded that they are reviewing their compensation policies to guarantee pay parity, focusing on gender due to the recent #MeToo and #TimesUp movements.

All of this is changing the way we talk about office politics, sexual harassment, and what is acceptable behavior in and out of the office. Everyone, women and men, deserves to be able to come to work without fear of sexual misconduct. And in order to know our value and communicate effectively, we have to be a part of this conversation.

The Elephant in the Room

In this chapter I want to have a real conversation about office politics and sexual harassment, so I have to address the elephant in the room—I am engaged to be married to my coworker.

Joe and I fell in love as peers, and our relationship was one in which neither of us felt pressured by power dynamics. The core of it is simple: I love him. And yes, we met at work.

I'm often asked "knowing" questions about Joe, with winks, sly smiles, or downright bawdy terms. Don't get me started on the Twitter comments. It is laughable to me how interested some people are in the personal lives of two fifty-something people. Intrusive questions are tossed at me, my friends, and my employees on a daily basis. My entire inner circle has received calls from the *National Enquirer* asking about the most intimate details of our relationship. I get asked constantly about my relationship with Joe.

Let me be boastful for a moment; I am the mother of two remarkable girls. I could stop there and die happy.

I am also a best-selling author, have been named one of the most powerful people in media, just celebrated ten years on a show with its highest ratings ever, am a 2018 Matrix award winner, and I started a nationwide women's empowerment community.

And I will be damned if every interview I give these days gets reduced to questions about Joe.

I don't owe all of my personal details to the world. Although many believe I do. For example, we did an interview with CBS's Lesley Stahl for *CBS Sunday Morning*. It was supposed to be on the ten-year anniversary of *Morning Joe*, Joe's music career, and my Know Your Value movement. Producers insisted that those were the three main topics of the piece and assured me that they are not a gossipy show. Then the cameras started rolling. Lesley must have asked me twenty different ways about my relationship with Joe. She spent most of the interview doing this. At one point, I asked if they could stop the interview. She looked at me slyly and said, "Nope, cameras are rolling." I was crestfallen, because she wanted background on my children. Her argument? Lesley said that the story is "out there," so it's "fair game."

No, actually it is not. I have never shared my story, because it is not mine alone and I can't speak for the others close to me. And no, it is not "out there," not even close. Having said that, the piece Lesley produced turned out well—it showed my discomfort and even my pain. But I felt really uncomfortable, first and foremost, for my family.

Speaking only for myself, here it is: here is our big splashy story. We fell in love. We hope to be married by the time this book is printed.

So on to #MeToo, which I hope thrives for my daughters. I want it to level the playing field. I want to have a conversation about how we can build better workplace cultures in which women are empowered to speak up every time they are harassed, devalued, or demeaned. So I did what I have done in every other chapter of this book and in all other books that I have written: I talked to other women and asked them to share their stories.

And this is a conversation that goes to the heart of knowing your value. According to a 2016 study by the Equal Employment Opportunity Commission as reported by the *New York Times*, when workers experiencing harassment were presented with multiple options on how they would approach the situation, the least common answer from both genders was to try to take a formal action of some kind.

According to the same report, approximately *three out of four* individuals who experienced harassment never spoke to a union representative, supervisor, or manager about the inappropriate conduct. You have a voice. This book is about empowering you to use that voice . . . and that 100 percent applies in situations where someone is abusing you or treating you inappropriately.

Your Employer Needs to Have Your Back

Shelley Zalis, CEO of The Female Quotient, stresses how crucial it is that employers are held accountable for creating workplace cultures where women are heard, respected, and safe. While things have clearly gotten off track, she has advice for how they can be rectified.

She tells me, "It is the responsibility of companies who created the environment to make a safe place where all employees feel that they belong. I think there needs to be accountability for all of those leaders that are in power. We need to show that there is punitive damage."

> *It is the responsibility of companies who created the environment to make a safe place where all employees feel that they belong.* —SHELLEY ZALIS

To do this, she recommends remembering what we learned as children, "If we didn't play nicely with one another in the schoolyard, we went to the principal's office and there were consequences. I think there need to be consequences for bad behavior and there also should be a reward for making the company better by calling out the issues, regardless of the levels where it's happening. There is a boss at every level, so even if it is something that the CEO is responsible for, that CEO has a boss too—their board!"

Not only punishing the people who behave badly, but rewarding the ones who are brave enough to speak out, is an easy change that could have a huge impact.

Shelley tells me, "No one today should get away with abusing power. I think there are plenty of things that we can do that encourage all employees to call it out when they see it, to call it out when they experience it. They should be rewarded for that and not feel like they are doing something wrong. We should create a lot of new policies inside of companies that allow all people to be their best selves and be able to rise to the top and feel safe in an environment that they can thrive in."

According to an executive summary from the co-chairs of the Equal Employment Opportunity Commission's Select Task Force on the Study of Harassment in the Workplace in June 2016, "Workplace culture has the greatest impact on allowing harassment to flourish, or conversely, in preventing harassment. The importance of leadership cannot be overstated—effective harassment prevention efforts, and workplace culture in which harassment is not tolerated, must start with and involve the highest level of management of the company.

"But a commitment (even from the top) to a diverse, inclusive, and respectful workplace is not enough. Rather, at all levels, across all positions, an organization must have systems in place that hold employees accountable for this expectation. Accountability systems must ensure that those who engage in harassment are held responsible in a meaningful, appropriate, and proportional manner, and that those whose job it is to prevent or respond to harassment should be rewarded for doing that job well (or penalized for failing to do so). Finally, leadership means ensuring that anti-harassment efforts are given the necessary time and resources to be effective."

Understanding that corporations share a huge responsibility in building a corporate structure where women are safe and feel comfortable to report is crucial. If you do not feel that your company is focused on building that for employees at your company, it should be time to start looking for a new job.

Understand the Purpose of the Meeting

As the senior vice president of Human Resources for Independence Blue Cross, Jeanie Heffernan has seen how difficult it has been for women to navigate in the workforce. During our interview for this book, she told me something that has resonated with me: understand the purpose behind every meeting on your calendar.

She tells me, "Just recently as an example, not even a colleague, but a board member of mine reached out to ask if I would like to have lunch with him and another male individual that he was wanting to introduce me to. I don't know this board member all that well, so I was just kind of like, okay, this is a little sensitive. You know, he is a board member and I have to manage the politics, but I also need to know what am I walking into, what am I getting in to?

"So I just sent back, 'I am happy to do that, can you help me understand what the purpose of the lunch is? What is it you need from me? What is your hope of the outcome of this introduction to this gentleman?' You can ask that question of any professional situation—breakfast, lunch, dinner, meeting, etcetera.

"It's always helpful to have clarity: Why are we there? What are we trying to accomplish? What are the expected outcomes? Whoever is being invited to the session should be clear about the purpose and the intended outcomes, so the meeting doesn't end up in awkwardness of some sort. You want everyone to understand the meeting is for the business purposes and not a social situation."

Jeanie's strategy allows her to avoid situations in which she could be made uncomfortable, but also allows her the opportunity to foster and build strong relationships with her colleagues.

It's always helpful to have clarity: Why are we there?
What are we trying to accomplish?
What are the expected outcomes?
—JEANIE HEFFERNAN

She elaborates, "You are going to be prepared and able to bring to the table your reflections, your thoughts, your input to whatever the topic is at hand so you are just not in a reactionary mode, but you are really crisp, prepared, and project yourself in a very positive, informed, and professional way."

Clarifying the purpose of every meeting makes them more productive for everyone. If there is no purpose behind the meeting, you should not feel any pressure to attend. We need to be on the lookout to align ourselves with people who will bring value to the table—on every level.

Being Your Own #1 Advocate

Shelley Zalis suggests that sometimes you can give men both the benefit of the doubt AND protect yourself. She recalls a story in which her boss—unknowingly—put her in an uncomfortable situation, and how she handled it. "When I was in my twenties living and working in New York City, I went to a dinner meeting with my boss in Connecticut. It was about 11 PM and he dropped me off at the train station to go back to the city. I spoke up and told him I wasn't comfortable taking a train at night, and that he would either have to drive me back or get a car to take me home. I wasn't trying to be rude, but I had to find my voice. My boss didn't realize that I felt unsafe—it was simply what he would have done himself. Give others the benefit of the doubt and, when something makes you uncomfortable at work, don't just hold it in—make them aware of your feelings."

*Give others the benefit of the doubt and, when something
makes you uncomfortable at work, don't just hold it in—
make them aware of your feelings.* –SHELLEY ZALIS

Repeat after me: when something makes you uncomfortable at work, don't just hold it in—make them aware of your feelings. I want to make this into a T-shirt and give it to every woman I know.

And sadly, Shelley wasn't the only person I spoke with who had an uncomfortable 11 PM interaction. Marcia Davies, chief operating officer for the Mortgage Bankers Association, tells me about a time when she too, had to speak up to protect herself. "I was on business travel staying at a hotel that I was doing a lot of business with at the time, and was stunned when the hotel's director of sales called my guest room at 11 PM to say he was getting the security pass key to come visit me. He was clearly intoxicated, and I was frightened, so I called security immediately.

"The next day we were both in a meeting, and I expected him to apologize for his behavior from the night before, but he did the opposite. He told me he was disappointed I felt the need to call security—wasn't I flattered by his interest in me? I calmly explained to him that he had lost the opportunity to work with my organization, and I had our account transferred to another sales person. I hope the loss of commission made him think twice about acting inappropriately with female clients."

In this situation, Marcia used her leverage as the client to financially impact the person who was sexually harassing her. I know that not everyone who finds themself in this type of situation has the same leverage. But I can't say this enough—communicating effectively is KEY to your professional development and your own well-being. And when you use your voice in potentially uncomfortable or unsafe work situations, you are truly being your own best advocate. You should never, under any circumstances, allow someone to undermine your value or your safety.

It Is About Power

It's easy to say, "Never go for drinks with your boss," or to view every colleague's offer of drinks as an improper solicitation. But like any other serious issue, we need to be careful that we don't allow criminal acts by a few to incite a witch hunt. People should not be tried by the media, but by courts of law or by Human Resources at their companies. And if we start viewing all men as potential sexual predators, we miss out on opportunities to connect with sponsors and mentors who can help grow our careers.

Shelley Zalis also knows that we need to be careful about overgeneralizing. She says, "I don't think [the current sensitivity about sexual politics at work] is about men and women, I think it is about power, and the majority of people in power are men, so it becomes a male issue. And I think the best mentors or sponsors are people who are not like you because that is how you learn and you grow. It is the whole thing of diversity; I think it does help us to be better when we get advice with different opinions, all around. It's about power. That power in the past has been very linear, and I think the power of today and the future is going to be very collaborative. Looking at more micropods of leadership will help us effect change on a more local level inside of big organizations."

I think the best mentors or sponsors are people who are not like you because that is how you learn and you grow. —SHELLEY ZALIS

Executive coach Liz Bentley explains how what has happened as a result of the Harvey Weinstein scandal has caused a positive shift in power. #MeToo and the power of the Women's Movement show that women are not backing down. She says, "As much as it's a hard time in the world for women, it's a great time in the world for women. The

Harvey Weinstein story, the abuse he committed, is so horrific and it's so fantastic that the stories have finally come out. There are probably a lot of guys right now who are really scared—and who should be."

Strength in Numbers

Liz Bentley knows that fostering a community of women who support each other is key to this equation—and that requires buy-in from women, and a recognition that sisterhood is powerful. She says, "Women are great just the way they are in many, many ways. One of the things they don't do well is support each other. Women are conditioned throughout their lives to really see things through a male's perspective. So recognize prejudice, and support women who are strong."

> *Women are conditioned throughout their lives to really see things through a male's perspective. So recognize prejudice, and support women who are strong.* —LIZ BENTLEY

Shelley Zalis believes in "the power of the pack" and knows that we are stronger when we work together. She tells me that she thinks the key to all of this is having safe spaces, where women are able to have these hard conversations together. "When you are with people that you know are supporting you, it is a lot easier to have those kinds of conversations and offer solutions."

And beyond finding safe spaces to have these authentic conversations, Shelley suggests that we reconsider how we talk about workplace training. "Right now, every company has been doing classic textbook stuff, which does not work. What about empathy training? What about training people to go back to the golden rule of do unto others as you would want done unto yourself? It is about respect in the workplace. I think we need to start talking about solutions that will work, and not just the classic ones that we have inherited. I think you find this in groups with like-minded individuals, with open-minded individuals, and with individuals that listen, and want to activate change. Not just bitch and moan about problems, but how do we create solutions that are next steps, that are not complicated, that we can keep doing this one and then this one and then this one?"

Using this solutions-oriented approach, Shelley is hopeful for the future. She says, "One day we can look back and say, 'Wow, look how far we have come, it is not that hard, it is not that scary,' actually, it is pretty easy when we break them into steps."

Talk to each other. Talk about what makes you uncomfortable. Find spaces like the Girls' Lounge, where you can feel safe to do this . . . or build your own.

And all of this leads to why I turned what I started here in the book into a national women's conference series and digital platform in the first place. I wanted to create an empowered community for women where they felt they had a voice. So that is what I did.

CHAPTER 11

STARTING A MOVEMENT
The Progression of Know Your Value

My story, with Katty Kay, Melody Barnes, Ashton Whitmoyer, Jennifer Condon, and Kasie Hunt

Growing the Value of Know Your Value

It started with this book. When it was first released back in 2011, women would come up to me at events, in the office, and even on the streets to tell me that they read *Know Your Value* and used the lessons to get a raise. From entry-level assistants to vice presidents at global companies, complete strangers would run up to me and jump up and down like they won *The Price Is Right*, exclaiming, "Oh my God! Oh my God! I read your book and I got a raise!" From the day this book was first released, I quickly learned women were hungry for the book's central message—that once you know your value and learn to express it, your value goes up and you see tangible results. But more needed to be done to get this message to as many women as possible.

Knowing what it is like to be undervalued, I wanted to create a movement that was relatable for all women. I had co-produced high-level women's conferences and had been one of those women on stage—either moderating or being interviewed.

BBC correspondent Katty Kay has also appeared at a number of women's conferences across the country, including my own, and when asked why she thought they were important, she told me, "Every year women are doing better in school than men. We're starting to earn more than our husbands (25 percent of American women now earn more than their husbands and the number is growing). But we're still not getting to the top in the numbers we should. In every industry, that's causing frustration and a boom in women's networks. We know more women makes for better outcomes, but we haven't figured out how to get there yet. These conferences are part of that puzzle, and I haven't yet been to a women's conference that the women themselves didn't find incredibly valuable."

Shelley Zalis, CEO of The Female Quotient, created The Girls' Lounge as a space for women to connect, collaborate, and activate change together. She wanted to form an environment that fosters new ideas and inspires action around diversity and leadership while creating a new culture for the leaders of tomorrow. Her team believes that the more we advocate for one another and embrace what makes women different, the better business and life will become. About the needs for these spaces for women, she tells me, "One person alone doesn't make shit happen; it is the power of the collective. We all have different strengths, and we complement each other."

Like me, her need to drive this conversation came from years of having to figure it out on her own. "I didn't really have that support system, which is why for me, the best thing I have ever done was to build The Girls' Lounge, because it has been the best support system I have ever had," Shelley explains.

Citing a pioneer in female empowerment, she says, "Gloria Steinem really says, 'I didn't start the movement, I inspired a movement.' A movement is a collective of people with the same purpose and the same passion. I really do believe that one of my greatest assets is not listening to what others tell me when they've said I am wrong and I have to be a certain way. I followed my heart to make my way the new way, which has worked for me and for the people around me."

One of our 2015 speakers, Melody Barnes, underscores the importance of engaging with other women on the topic of self-empowerment: "They say you have to hear something seven times before it sinks in; hearing that message over and over—and from different perspectives—is really important for women. You never know when someone is dealing with a challenge, and when they hear a message at the right time and in a way that resonates, it helps them confront the issue."

> *You never know when someone is dealing with*
> *a challenge, and when they hear a message*
> *at the right time and in a way that resonates,*
> *it helps them confront the issue.* —MELODY BARNES

The success of the first edition of *Know Your Value* inspired me to step into the world of women's events myself, but I wanted to bring something new to the table. Many of the important events I took part in lacked a key component: accessibility. A sense that any woman could change her life right there and then. I wanted to offer tangible tips. The basics. I wanted to offer advice and inspiration they could put into practice the moment they walked out the door.

The Grow Your Value Bonus Competition

I decided to go back to my roots as I geared up to take this tremendous risk. Many years ago, I was an anchor in Hartford, Connecticut. I have incredible friends there who I knew would simply love this message. I picked up the phone and called Diane Smith and Duby McDowell, who were my on-air colleagues back in the day. Soon after we recruited Robyn Gengras, and together we produced the very first pilot Know Your Value event in Hartford, Connecticut. (By the way, I did not ask NBC if I could do this. For so many reasons the answer would have been "no.")

I drove my team crazy. I obsessed 24/7 over the preparations for this one event. I wanted to recreate my book in real life on stage and I wanted women in the audience to feel as good as when they had read the book. I recruited the great Gayle King as the keynote and we found sponsorships in companies like Aetna and TIAA-CREF. We operated as if we were running a campaign, working the phones and knocking on doors. What we discovered is that those three words—"Know Your Value"—generated interest, willing speakers, and momentum.

We were weeks away from the event at the Marriott Renaissance in downtown Hartford and it was coming together, but I felt something was missing. I wanted women to actually see and feel the process of knowing your value. I wanted them to leave the room that day owning it. I didn't feel like we had completely nailed it yet. But on one of my five-mile runs, a light bulb went off over my head. I immediately called Duby. "Two things! We have to have them. A live gospel choir and a competition!" I was panting. I could imagine the thought bubble over Duby's head, "Mika's lost her mind." Duby nixed the gospel choir, but as she heard me talking a hundred miles an hour about the competition, she knew I wasn't going to let this go. We had just weeks to work out the legalities and details, but I was determined to get it done.

The competition turned out to be the heart and soul of Know Your Value's debut event. I convinced my old TV station, WFSB Channel 3 in Hartford, to let me make an announcement "selfie-style" on my iPhone. "Hey there Hartford, it's Mika Brzezinski, remember me? I invite you to join me Monday, May 6 at the Marriott Renaissance in downtown Hartford for the very first Know Your Value event. I want to teach you not only to KNOW your value, but to communicate it effectively, so come join us—and while you're at it, take part in the KNOW YOUR VALUE/GROW YOUR VALUE BONUS COMPETITION!! It's so easy. Make a video just like me on your phone in selfie mode and tell me in a minute or less what your value is and why YOU deserve a $10,000 bonus. Five of you will be chosen as finalists and we will work with you to help you pitch your value on stage. The winner will get $10,000 on the spot."

Submissions started pouring in. Women from all walks of life. Women who were relaunching their careers after having kids. From CEOs to women starting businesses. Women who had been fired, dumped, or just plain unappreciated. Women even sent in submissions from prison! We knew this was it. THIS was our way of SHOWING women the process of truly understanding their value and putting it into words. We picked five amazing finalists and got to work.

We enlisted professional coaches from the Hartford area like Liz Bentley, Kendra Farn, and Diane Smith. Diane and I have since published a book together. She also helped me deliver my second child nineteen years ago. Like I said, I have some amazing friends in Hartford! Soon, the event we were creating revolved around the competition. While Gayle King and Katty Kay and especially those three words, KNOW YOUR VALUE, may have been the draw that got us a sold-out audience of 500 women, we were able to introduce the contestants throughout the day and have them share their stories in between the important conversations on stage about negotiating and health.

The audience got to know contestants like Darcy Sordo and her coach Kendra Farn. Darcy was fired from a big job in New York and had started a secondhand store in Madison, Connecticut, which had become a local hub for moms. Her pitch was all about using the money to build a website, and she was amazing. (She also had a small white tube coming out of her sleeve near her shoulder—more on that later.) There was a contestant from Avon, Connecticut, who was recently divorced and she had wanted to build an exercise studio in her basement so she could make money while still looking after her girls. And who could forget the mother of eight from the North End of Hartford who wanted to open an animal sanctuary.

There was also Jennifer Hotchkiss, who was working as an administrative assistant in Berlin, Connecticut. She has great posture and a fantastic voice. She was young, scared, and hungry. You could feel it. As she stared at me across the stage, her eyes were intense. She was a woman with little to lose and she was putting it all out there. Shaking, she shared that she was a single mom, with no college degree. That she was tired of being left out in the world. That she wanted to be the boss someday. She also conceded that she knew she had to get a college degree in order to have a chance at a better life. She wanted to be the first person in her family to go to college. For her own reasons, she mentioned Bay Path University in Longmeadow, Massachusetts. Her pitch was raw and real. She almost won the competition.

In the end, Darcy Sordo was the clear winner. She was fabulous, heartfelt, fun, and focused all at the same time. As she hugged me on stage, I asked her about that tube. "Oh my gosh," she said, "I had heart surgery forty-eight hours ago! My doctor didn't want me to come but I just could not miss this! I KNOW MY VALUE, MIKA! I was practicing my pitch on the stretcher!" That should just about say it all about how compelling women found this idea of knowing their value.

But then something remarkable happened. We announced Jennifer Hotchkiss as the runner-up. All the contestants got a check for their time—because time is money—and as I was explaining this to the audience, an elegant-looking lady started pulling at my skirt. Robyn and Duby, the producers of the event, started closing in on her, worried I was about to be assaulted in some way.

That woman was the chief marketing officer for Bay Path University.

She grabbed the microphone and all of a sudden it felt like we were all in a movie, and she was the main event. "You are all winners," she said, as she introduced herself. "But you, young lady (pointing at Jennifer), you are WONDERFUL. Come see me on Monday, we are going to get you that degree." She gave Jennifer a full scholarship on the spot. The room melted. Tears were everywhere. Talk about a moment when I knew this movement was real. That moment has driven me ever since.

That special moment—when Jennifer advocated for herself so fiercely, and was rewarded so quickly—has driven Jennifer too, and changed the course of her life. She put herself out there, took a chance, and wow. Jennifer remembers those first conversations with the university with awe. "I ended up talking to them and they were going to give me $12,000 to finish my bachelor's in three years. I went back to them and said, 'Can I do it in two?' And they said, 'You really want to do it in two?' and I said, 'This is the goal I have set for myself. Let's do it in two.'"

This was not a woman who was willing to wait for things to be given to her. This was a woman who was ready to fight for herself. Jennifer then signed up immediately for classes in leadership and organizational studies—exactly what she had promised to do on stage. In May of 2016, Jennifer Hotchkiss graduated summa cum laude and was even the commencement speaker at her graduation.

In her speech, she went back to where it all began.

"At my commencement speech, I brought it back full circle to the Know Your Value Conference, when I asked for that bonus. I talked about *The Wizard of Oz* and the yellow brick road and how it takes you on so many twists and turns. I ended it with Frank L. Baum's quote, 'You always had the power, my dear, you just had to learn it for yourself.'"

Boy, did Jennifer take that lesson and run with it. She took the spirit of Know Your Value and she ran with it too, and her life has been fuller as a result. She describes some of the more interesting changes in her life: "I'm working, I'm a mom, and I'm writing. I write every day. While I was at school, I got published twice. I got published in a textbook and then *The Huffington Post* published my speech and put the video up during their graduation special for 2016." Jennifer has lived her dreams, and that all started with her picking up her phone and making that one-minute video.

Growing that Brand

I was on to something. I was also ready to present my idea to my boss, Phil Griffin, and Pat Fili-Krushel, then head of NBCUniversal. Phil and I were in a completely different place now, and Phil is the first to say it. Phil was one of the first people I circled back to and interviewed again for the re-publication of this book. He recalls, "I remember the first Know Your Value event I went to and how connected everybody in that audience was to you. . . . When you see something like that, you can't help but be in awe of the message. This is real, this is game-changing, and that audience was gripped by it. "

I was amazed to hear that Phil felt he had grown from our experience together as much as I had. We both used those learning experiences to be better at our jobs. And more than just growing as a boss and friend to me, he was one of the first people on an executive level at NBC to champion the Know Your Value message as a movement and a business. He did this for a number of reasons, but the primary one was that he believed in me.

Phil explains, "I had a top talent who connected with our world. You gave birth to it, made the case for it, and it made sense. And I truly believe it made you better on TV. It wasn't actually taking time away from TV; it was helping build your confidence, your voice, and who you are on air."

Or, as Phil put it, "You were better at TV and more confident, as you dug deep into this new project and understood it."

It is true—for five years, I dug deep and built this thing. It will always be my proudest professional accomplishment.

So in partnership with the network that built *Morning Joe*, we took our Know Your Value message on the road. We have been to cities all around the country: Chicago, Boston, Orlando, D.C., Philadelphia, Hartford, and New York, and have met with women from all walks of life. In addition to getting to meet so many of the amazing attendees, I have been honored to share the stage with some of the most inspiring women I know: Martha Stewart, Senator Elizabeth Warren, Hoda Kotb, Senator Claire McCaskill, Amy Cuddy, Katty Kay, Laura Brown, Vanessa Deluca, Sarah Jessica Parker, Janine Driver, Jane Pauley, and so many more.

And after the election, we took the business to the next level and expanded into custom corporate events and programs, and a website that works as an online resource hub and community for women. All of this with support from my bosses, who know my value and believe in me. This book has transformed into something much larger than words on paper or a conference series. We are an empowered community, ready to take our careers and our lives to the next level.

Your Value Is More Than Money

The bonus competition at my conferences compels women to develop a skill that they often think does not apply to their work lives. When I ask women to come up with a reason why they're worth a $10,000 bonus, I'm asking them to dig deep. To find out what their passions are and express them fully. Articulate what has broken them and what has made them stronger. Do a full MRI of their souls to try and put into words what they really want out of life. We often think it's either inappropriate to mix these kinds of intense feelings with our work life, or we just don't have the time to think that deeply about what we want. But if we don't take the time to dig deep and get to the heart of what motivates us, we are "leaving money on the table" at work, and in all our relationships.

Because it's not just about money. The Know Your Value process and "digging deep" is about discovering yourself and finding your true calling so that it is much easier to articulate something that you are passionate about. You can grow your worth through leadership roles and new opportunities that do not necessarily translate right away into financial gain. And if you improve your life and find out who you are and what you are made of, and if you can put it into words, the rest will follow. ALL of our contestants come out of the process with a renewed sense of their worth.

Ashton Dug Deep

Ashton Whitmoyer did not win the $10,000 prize, but just like Jennifer Hotchkiss, she ultimately gained so much more.

As a small-business owner from Lititz, Pennsylvania, Ashton was a minor celebrity in her own community when she first saw information about the contest circulating on social media. She explained, "I thought, 'What the heck, I'll give it a chance and do it. I have fought to make a name for myself, living in the community I lived in, being so young and an entrepreneur.' Because of that, I really felt I had a handle on what my value was and what I brought to the town. That is what ultimately made me submit that one-minute video, because I was confident in who I was and what I could offer in the workplace."

But what Ashton did not yet realize, as a young woman just starting her career, was that there was so much she needed to learn about her value. "The biggest takeaway for me was to always be true to my-self and who I am, and that who I am has nothing to do with what people think of me or who people want me to be. It's really being true to myself and what I want out of life and having the confidence to si-lence the voices of doubt that surround us," she told me when I asked what she gained from the experience. Starting her own business at a young age had left her feeling accomplished without having taken the time to think about her long-term goals. Her coaches helped Ashton look at her life and really address what was holding her back from feeling successful.

> *The biggest takeaway for me was to always be true to myself and who I am, and that who I am has nothing to do with what people think of me or who people want me to be.* —ASHTON WHITMOYER

Ashton took her loss in the competition and ran with it. The expe-rience had inspired her to be gutsy.

"I said, 'Okay, I said I was going to do all these things if I won the $10,000, so now I'm just going to do it without the money.' The first step I took was that I decided I was going to go back to school, so I ap-plied to Penn State to get my master's degree in Community Psychol-ogy and Social Change in the fall of 2015. That was the first best step for me and something I could physically do to start to make these changes in my life. I also hired an employee to help me run my boutique, which is something else that I said I wanted to do in my pitch."

In addition to going back to school, Ashton used a dramatic expe-rience in college as a catalyst. She spoke about an abusive relationship in her pitch on stage in Philadelphia. She dug deep for her pitch and drummed up the confidence to tell her story on stage in Philadelphia and shared her desire to speak to young people about the value of healthy relationships. That moment changed everything for Ashton.

She also realized, while examining her understanding of her value, that her marriage was no longer working. "Through this experience, I have also realized the relationships I had to sever in my life, whether it be friendships or my own marriage." On how her experience at the conference led to her making such dramatic life changes, she explained, "This movement helped me to know my value and what I want in life, and not just in my career but in my personal life. Before *Know Your Value*, I didn't have a voice. I didn't have a voice to stand up for what I wanted, and I didn't have a voice to make my opinions, thoughts, and ideas known. After the experience, I had a voice that I couldn't silence and I realized that I didn't want to silence it, and I needed to be true to myself. My biggest life change since the experience was my divorce. It was very hard for me to have such a painful experience be so public in a small town.

"I look back a few years ago in 2015, and I don't even recognize that person, and when I see that initial sixty-second video I submitted, I'm like, 'I don't even know who that is.' I thought I was this confident person submitting this video, because I thought that I had it figured out and I knew my worth. I discovered it by opening my own business at age twenty-two. I thought I could take on the world. Going through this experience made me realize that being confident is so much more than putting on an outward appearance. You have to really be honest with yourself and who you want to be, and quiet the voice of doubt that surrounds you in society. There is so much in life that you are missing out on if you only do the comfortable things. It takes a giant dose of being uncomfortable in order to live an authentic and meaningful life. It changed every aspect of my life, and it was the push I needed to get into [Community Psychology] and create change in my community. I know that this is just the beginning for me, but I am doing the fulfilling work that I so craved. I knew point A, and I knew point B, and Mika and the Know Your Value team helped me get from one to the other."

Women Helping Women

Katty Kay is a brand on her own, but she has always been eager to participate any time I have an ask for Know Your Value. She has participated as a speaker at a number of our events on our national tour and was quick to contribute to this book. When asked why she was willing to take so much of her time to help with my business, she answers, "KYV and *The Confidence Code* are inextricably linked. Why do women undervalue themselves? It's often because their perception of their ability is out of whack with their actual ability—they don't think they are as good as they actually are. This is why they hold back from going for risk assignments, why they don't raise their hands in key meetings, and why they don't ask for their true value in terms of compensation. Through the course of a woman's career, it means they hold themselves back from reaching their full potential. Our research isn't the same, our methods aren't always the same, our advice isn't always the same—but our fundamental belief that women deserve to go farther, do more, be better rewarded is totally in synch. Plus, the conferences are great fun and you meet wonderful women—and I got to take my daughter."

> *Our research isn't the same, our methods aren't always the same, our advice isn't always the same—but our fundamental belief that women deserve to go farther, do more, be better rewarded is totally in synch.* —KATTY KAY

One of the many reasons I love having Katty as an important member of the Know Your Value community is that she consistently steps up for the women who fill her circle. She is an active participant in conversations about how to advance women.

After the BBC released its annual salary report in July 2016 and disclosed that two-thirds of its highest salaries were given to men, Katty joined with forty other high-profile BBC employees in an open letter urging her employers to close the pay gap. She is unafraid to stick her neck out for both herself and her colleagues, and she serves as an example of the ways we can support one another.

MSNBC correspondent Kasie Hunt was someone I knew, immediately upon meeting her, had talent. But I also knew she needed help, and that I wanted to help her. From hair (hers was a mop! It got in the way of her message) to helping advocate for her at the executive level, I fought for her as hard as I had ever fought for myself.

She explained to my editor, "I have mentored a lot of reporters and have had coffee with interns who want to know, 'Hey, how can I move up? What should I be doing or be focused on?' I think working with Mika has sort of underscored the point to me that it is important to have [mentors], specifically women, who are mentors to other women. I think I have always tried to be helpful to people who ask for my help, regardless of their gender or their background."

She explains how this experience has affected her: "I try to be more thoughtful about going out of my way to help other women, but also acknowledging that that's a reality in the workplace and in journalism. When people ask for my thoughts . . . I think you can easily ignore it and say, 'Hey, we face the same challenges in the workplace as men do!' But I think, to be perfectly honest, I don't think that's true. I have a lot of mentors to whom I owe a lot, both men and women, but if I didn't have a woman who was such a strong mentor, I would be in a very different place than I am now."

No One Has It Figured Out

When I started spreading the Know Your Value message, I needed to make sure that I was not presenting myself as an expert on everything. That is why I have sought out the aspirational women and men who speak at my conferences, contribute to my books, and write for my website. What works for one of us might not work for the whole, and it is more than okay to take the time to seek out the voices that are most helpful to you and then re-adjust yourself. Your brand will grow throughout your career, and that will mean course-correcting from time to time.

Melody Barnes spoke at one of our Know Your Value events, but found herself listening to the other speakers of the day during her downtime. As someone who is constantly striving to become a better version of herself, she took a step back and viewed the day from the lens of a participant. And she found that the message was one she could apply to herself.

She remembers, "It wasn't long after [the Know Your Value event] that a company asked me to consider a project, and they wanted a lot . . . a whole lot of time and work. And I thought, 'We can negotiate a figure that I know they would accept and they would hire me, but it wouldn't be the real value that I was going to give them. So, I am going to say what I think this is worth and what I am worth, knowing full well there is more than a 50/50 chance that they are going to say no.' Mika's message was that you must be comfortable with the fact that people are going to say no, and I walked in knowing that."

I was happy to know that Melody had used the advice to advocate for herself, prepared that the answer might not go in her favor. She was happy with the result and told me, "They did say no, but I was completely comfortable with that. I think I was more comfortable with that outcome than if I had undersold myself and they had said yes."

And when I asked her if there was anything else she gained from participating in the Know Your Value message, she said, "I think the bottom line in knowing your value is knowing yourself, and that lens can help you navigate the future. It helps you understand your ultimate objectives and make decisions about what's right for you personally and professionally, as opposed to what's right for others. Or what others think you should do, or the narrative you've created for yourself that's inconsistent with your core values and goals. I've also found it works best when I've made career choices and professional choices that are integrated with one another; you've found the sweet spot when there's alignment."

A Universal Message

Of the many wonderful surprises I have found as I have taken the Know Your Value message on the road, one of the most significant is how our message is transformative to more than just women. When I first wrote this book, I talked about how my experiences were central to what many other women were facing. But as I traveled the country, formed partnerships with diversity and inclusion teams at different companies, and talked to attendees at events, I realized that most of these issues are universal.

Knowing how to speak up authentically when feeling less-than-empowered is something that all of us must learn to do in the workplace. I have spoken with multicultural men's groups, the LGBTQ community, and various minority associations, and they have all told me the same thing: They need help in getting to the point where they feel their unique voice matters.

Phil Griffin agreed that his work community needed buy-in from the front office. It was one of the main reasons he chose to invest in the program as a business. He explains, "The great thing about Know Your Value is that it is not gender-specific. That said, I understand why the message resonates with women the way it does. Your message is especially relevant for women because the environment is so much harder for women. I think I've understood that when dealing with on-air talent, because I make the effort to understand all of their challenges.

I've made sure I spend time with younger people who are growing up through the system and make sure that they are given the time to adjust to their work environment and have people in the front office who understand what they need to succeed."

Melody Barnes explained that having open conversations about confidence and women knowing their value can be especially helpful for women of color.

"African-American women often face challenges when they are questioned about their appearance, how they dress, how they present themselves, how they wear their hair, and even whether that hair is natural or not! So many African-American women at all stages of their career have come up to me simply because I wear my hair naturally now and say, 'Wow, I've been wanting to do that, but I don't know if I could do it in a professional setting.' They ask me, 'How do you get that confidence?' You must always ask yourself what's right for you at a particular moment in your career. What I tell people is that I trust my professional barometer and this is who I am. If I can't show up at work as myself, then that is not a place where I want to be. I wear my natural hair at meetings of corporate boards and large nonprofit boards: in the private, public, and nonprofit sectors. I know not every woman has choices, but whenever possible, women need to be true to who they are, regardless of where they find themselves."

We have already discussed the pressure women feel to look a certain way, the efforts we should make to blend our appearance with our brand, and the times we should confidently embrace who we are regardless of what society expects. Finding the perfect look is still impossible for me, even after fifty years of trying. But the most important tip I can give you on your "look" as well as your life is to go in the direction that feels like the most natural fit. You've heard it before. I'll say it again: be yourself, because that is what you do best. You can't show other people your value if you can't even be yourself.

You can't show other people your value if you can't even be yourself. —MIKA BRZEZINSKI

Moving Forward

Know Your Value is more than a book, workshop, or conference meeting for me. It is my way of life. After spending years questioning my every move, looking to others for approval, questioning whether I belonged at my workplaces, and whether I was worth enough to others to ask for a pay raise, I have found myself at a place in my life where I know the only way for me to keep moving forward is by leaving my insecurities behind. Traveling around the country over the past several years talking about women knowing their value has allowed me to connect with so many remarkable people and gain strength from them as I share my own life story. We should continue to strive to be an empowered community of women who support each other by sharing lessons that we have learned the hard way and guiding others in the direction that will lead to personal fulfillment and professional success.

Given the challenges confronting women in Washington and across the world, knowing your value is more important today than ever. Women have made great strides through the years, but even before this current administration took over the White House, many of our friends and professional peers had trouble identifying their value in the workplace and fighting for the salaries they deserved. What is true in the age of Trump was true when he was still a struggling reality TV star. We women are too often prisoners of our own fears and self-imposed limitations. We must transcend those limits placed upon us by others and be fearless advocates for ourselves in our offices and at the negotiating table. If we are not, that lack of confidence will cost us money. We owe it to ourselves and the loved ones we support to do better. And we will!

The women and men whom I interviewed for this book believe that things will only get better for women in the future, despite the political and societal challenges that are buffeting us every day. Even those who see men as negative forces holding women back believe that they will soon have no choice but to recognize that the world has forever changed.

"I think we are making progress, and I think that progress is amplified by men having more strong, empowered daughters," Valerie Jarrett tells me. She flourished in her career when she worked for Mayor Daley, whom she describes as a supportive father and a husband to a strong wife. Valerie also notes that President Obama was the son of a strong single mom, the husband to a successful attorney, and the father of two independent daughters who always speak their minds. Barack Obama has always been surrounded by strong women, has valued them, and never failed to lift them up as examples.

Other women I interviewed spoke of the need for trailblazing women who could take leadership roles in fields traditionally dominated by men. Finance has long been controlled by men, as well as emerging fields like technology, which continues to be an ever-expanding center of economic power.

"What's astonishing and quite disturbing is at the top of the capitalist pyramid there are almost no women," Chrystia Freeland says. "The areas where the real money and power reside are still occupied almost exclusively by men."

Freeland covered the global economy for several decades as a reporter and editor of the *Financial Times*. In her past life, she was the global editor-at-large for Reuters, who has often appeared on *Morning Joe* to talk about the world economy, business, and politics. While sitting with Freeland on our studio set one day, I mentioned my plans to write the first edition of this book. She was instantly supportive of the concept because of the need for women to "hear the truth." That truth, says Freeland, is that when a job is high-status, society still defines it as male. "How many would picture a Wall Street titan in a skirt?" she asks. Freeland sees the same thing developing in the American science and technology industries right now.

"Most of the gain in income and productivity for the whole economy over the past decade, even the past couple of decades, is in the top 1 percent, and that's where the women aren't penetrating," she says. "I want to see women coming up with something and creating it and building it. I want a female Sergey Brin, I want a female John Paulson. I think there are lots of women out there. We need to create a culture that encourages that more. Think about the great tech start-ups— think Apple, Microsoft, Google, Facebook. Where are the girls coming up with these great ideas in their Harvard dorm rooms?"

I want to see women coming up with something and creating it and building it. —CHRYSTIA FREELAND

That is an important question that needs to be addressed by women in boardrooms and in positions of power. Fortunately, Freeland is in a position to help the cause because she is now Canada's Minister of Foreign Affairs.

As for me, I am still happily on the set of *Morning Joe* where I first met Minister Freeland as well as my future husband. It has been seven years since I wrote the first edition of this book, and over a decade since *Morning Joe* was launched in 2007. While much has changed in my life, the need to remain focused on forwarding the conversation of women getting their value is more vital than ever.

These can be confusing times for women in the workplace. With the Age of Trump colliding headfirst with the emerging #MeToo moment, it remains our challenge to keep talking to one another, supporting one another, and finally getting this right. It is on us to learn to communicate clearly and effectively and then use our voices loudly and clearly. And we must always remember that men must be a big part of that conversation. There is no need for us to waste time simply talking to ourselves.

And we must do more than just resist. We must recognize our value, engage our opponents, and prevail in the battle to do what is right. I love that women are running for office and voting in greater numbers at the polls; it is long past time that we know our value and drain the swamp of retrogrades and reactionaries who think it is still 1950. We live in a new era where harassed women no longer live in the shadows and where arrogant bosses cannot continue to hold women back from positions that are rightfully theirs simply because the guy in the front office holds antiquated views of a woman's place in society. The times, they are a-changing, and we must never let anyone in our lives think they can turn the clock back.

Resist

It is a word that has grown to mean more than a simple command. It has now evolved into a hashtag, a rallying cry, a political movement, and a guiding principle for millions who fear that America is losing its way day by day. But if you count yourself among the millions of "resisters," let me humbly suggest that regardless of your political affiliation, you and I owe more to our daughters, granddaughters, sisters, and friends than being nothing more than part of a collection of defiant acts. We women must start demanding more from our leaders in Washington, just as we must demand more from our bosses in the workforce. We must know our value, we must fight for our value, and we must actively work to replace those politicians and CEOs who choose to push back on the progress that those who have gone before us have already gained through blood, sweat, toil, and tears.

During his first year in the White House, Donald Trump has shown a shocking disregard for appointing women in leadership positions around Washington. The numbers paint a bleak picture of just how low our standing has slid under the new administration. Of all the judges and U.S. Attorneys Donald Trump nominated throughout 2017, more than 90 percent were men. Inside the White House, the president's first two chiefs of staff, two national security advisors, Secretary of State, Defense Secretary, Treasury Secretary, and the Attorney General, and every other senior position at 1600 Pennsylvania Avenue have been held by men. And let's face it. The few women who Trump keeps in close proximity have no governmental experience and are never around when men are making the most important decisions for this "Mad Men" administration.

If there is any silver lining to this gloomy political climate, it is that the situation is so challenging that women across America—and the rest of the world—have been awakened to the threats this administration poses, both in and out of government. So, Resist if this is what you believe to be the right thing to do. More importantly, it is time to fight with all of our might to get what we deserve in our workplace, in our homes, and in our personal lives, regardless of who is sitting in the White House. Do not be discouraged, do not ease up, and for heaven's sake, do not give in.

Now is the time to stand up and make a difference in any way you can. Support those women who are running for office in record numbers and know that when they get elected next year, we will finally be moving toward electing America's first woman president. The writing is on the wall. Women are the coming revolution in politics and the work world. I was so inspired by the women across Virginia who stood for hours in the driving rain to vote in the latest governor's race—all there to send a message to the Trump White House. Political analysts like my cohost said that it was women who made the difference in electing Virginia's governor. And I know that women will shape elections this year and for years to come, until such time that men in the White

House and on Capitol Hill understand that we will not be pushed to the side anymore.

Women have such special value. We prove it every day at work. We show it again when we get home, and again when we take care of our aging parents, when we give our children everything that we have left, and then we somehow dig even deeper to go the extra mile for that special person in our life.

Since you give everything you have to others, doesn't it make sense that you should stop once in a while to make sure that someone gives that value back to you? Of course, the answer is Yes! Yes. YES! Like many have over the past several years, I truly hope that you can use this book to start getting everything that you deserve in every part of your life! The time has passed that we leave "money on the table," whether at your job, in your home, or with the person whom you love the most. Know your value. Get it. And finally live the life that you deserve.

INDEX

abuse of power, 197, 201

Academy of Motion Picture Arts and Sciences, 191

Acio, Lorie, 166, 192

Administrative Science Quarterly, on importance of social ties in business, 132–133

Aetna, 208

African American women and Know Your Value message, 221

Alcindor, Yamiche, 62

alliances, 127–134

Anderson, Cameron, 71

anger, 24, 82, 174

Anthony, Lysette, 191

appearance, 178–180

assertiveness and acceptable behavior, 71

authenticity, 70–71, 221

Autodesk, 44

Babcock, Linda, 40, 84

backlash, 71, 77, 99–100, 141

Bair, Sheila
being heard by men, 100
on emotionalism in workplace, 81–83
in *Know Your Value* first edition, 7

mentors, 128–129

rejection of women's ideas, 97

self-promotion, 93–95

talking about family at work, 141–143

warning about subprime mortgage crisis, 62–64

Banfield, Ashleigh, 18

bargaining
acceptable behavior, 78
asking for a raise, 108–113
asking for more than is offered, 114–115
being ready to walk, 118–120
knowing the market value of your contributions, 104–107
persistence, 115–117
playing the victim, 32
rejection, 117–118, 219
relational account, 78
timing, 107

Barnes, Melody
being true to who you are, 221
engaging with other women about self-empowerment, 207
in *Know Your Value* first edition, 7
saying no, 219